# are you a DISCIPLE?

## SAYING YES TO A LIFE BEYOND CASUAL CHRISTIANITY

AN 8-WEEK BIBLE STUDY FOR WOMEN

Laurie Cole

**Production Coordinator** • Pam Henderson
**Layout and Design** • Pam Henderson, Emily Gentiles
**Editors** • Emily Ryan, Ada Burk
**Cover Design and Graphic Artwork** • Emily Seith, Emily Gentiles

*Priority Ministries*
Encouraging Women to Give God Glory & Priority

711 West Bay Area Boulevard, Suite 214, Webster, Texas 77598-4000
www.priorityministries.org

# Dedication

This study is dedicated to Pam Henderson, a true disciple of Jesus Christ, a modern-day Priscilla (Acts 18), and my beloved co-worker in ministry. Her wisdom, counsel, generosity, and godly example are an inspiration to Priority Ministries and to all who are privileged to know her—including and especially me. I love you, Pam.

# Acknowledgments

Laurie and the entire Priority Ministries staff wish to express our deep appreciation and gratitude to every woman who participated in the original pilot of *Are You a Disciple?* at **Sagemont Church in Houston, Texas,** in 2014. Each week these wonderful women provided us with evaluations and feedback that enabled us to improve and strengthen this study for you. As you review the following list of their names, we trust you will thank the Lord for each and every one of them.

Betsy Thompson, *Women's Minister*
Shari McCormack, *Women's Ministry Assistant*
Meghan Garrett, *Director, Mothering Matters Bible Study*
Peggy Hartenstein, *Director, LifeTouch Bible Study*
Tamara Skeete, *Director, M&M Bible study*
Pat Godwin, *Director, M&M Bible study*
Eloisa Torres & Patsie Guel, *Directors, Spanish Bible Study*
Cathy Ingram, *Director, Women of Hope Bible Study*

| | | | |
|---|---|---|---|
| Stevetta Abron | Susanna Blanchard | Martha Camp | Rosemarie Cotter |
| Debbie Adams | Judy Boessling | Doris Campbell | Vicki Covey |
| Rhonda Addison | Brenda Bondy | Danielle Campbell | Michelle Cox |
| Bea Aguilera | Tarshia Boutte | Donna Campbell | Julie Craddock |
| Josie Aguirre | Sharon Bouvier | Sandy Canion | Maria Crake |
| Connie Alameda | Paula Box | Sandy Canion | Teri Crawford |
| Nancy Alexander | Debbie Boyer | Maria Y. Cantu | Liz Crowell |
| karen Alford | Kathi Bradley | Lisa Caputo | Lesa Curl |
| Carolyn Alvarez | Laura Braly | Cathy Carlson | Amy Curtis |
| Angie Amyx | Christine Bridges | Tami Carroll | Jessica Cuthbert |
| Heather Armitage | Radien Brizendine | Rose Castillo | Olivia Daugherty |
| Angela Autrey | Shelly Brock | Sherial Caswell | Chiquita Davis |
| Denise Bacon | Sandra Brock | Mendy Caviness | Verna De George |
| Elena Baeza | Nancy Brooks | Yolanda Cerda | Sarah De Leon |
| Sarah Baker | Debbie Brooks | Mikelle Challenger | Konnie Decherd |
| Mary Baker | Linda V. Brown | Sheila Cheatwood | Jackie Decosmo |
| Elaine Baker | Stacy Brown | Nissa Choate | Kathy deLeon |
| Sheila Ball | Carol Brown | Dawn Christian | JoAnn Delgado |
| Donna Ball | Marsha Brown | Diane Church | Deborah Deloach |
| Tami Barbour | Debbie Brown | Jan Clark | Christina Denham |
| Dana Barnett | Diane Brownhill | Diddy Clark | Esperanza Diaz |
| Sarah Barnett | Kim Brummett | Anita Clark | Mary Jo Dittmar |
| Sharon Bass | Theresa Buckner | Leslie Clay | Verna Dobbs |
| Mary Bell | Summer Bullock | Connie Clemente | Glenda Dougharty |
| Debbie Bennett | Diane Burcham | Kimberly Coker | Zdenka Doyle |
| Megan Bennett | Ada Burk | Shannon Cole | Traci Dvorak |
| Sharon Berry | oy Burkhalter | Jacqueline Colunga | Dolly Edge |
| Alexis Bertsch | Cathleen Burkland | Krysta Connolly | Evelyn Edigin |
| Krystal Bettilyon | Jo Burnight | Annette Conwell | Tricia Ehman |
| Melissa Bittick | Imogene Butler | Kathy Corbett-Huff | Mary Ella Elam |
| JoAnn Blair | Patti Bynum | Laura Cornman | Paula Elkins |
| Barbara Blake | J Valerie Callahan | Pam Costales | Belinda Ellis |

| | | | |
|---|---|---|---|
| Kimberly Ellsworth | Rosalinda Gomez | Debbie Hubenak | Kirsten Leeper |
| Marty Engvall | Sara Gonzales | Wendy Huffman | Sandra Lengefeld |
| Libby Escalante | Gloria Gonzalez | Maryann Hutchison | Susan Levy |
| Kim Everett | Mona Gonzalez | Allene Izaguirre | Laurie Lindquester |
| Marilyn Evers | Susie Gorman | Frances Jackson | Kim Lindquist |
| Leslie Fair | Mona Graham | Sandra Jackson | Alexis Lochner |
| Melinda Fairey | Trace Griesel | Sandra Jacobs | Michelle Lockwood |
| Janice Farris | Karoline Griesel | Melanie Jacobson | Jennifer Lowrance |
| Becky Feezel | Mary Guel | Lara Jaime | Vicky Lucchese |
| Vilma I. Fernandez | Nancy Guevara | Tiana Jaime-Perez | Jean Maciukiewicz |
| Karla Fernandez | Angelita Guevara | Candy Jard | Tammi Mallory |
| Cay Ferrell | Brenda Guzman | Linu John | Donna Manahan |
| Jean Fibranz | Amy Gwin | Judy Johnson | Anita Mapes |
| Mary Jane Fitch | Kimberly Haddock | Brenda Johnson | Renea Marchi |
| Adelina Flores | Paula Hagan | Becki Johnson | Sammie Maricelli |
| Michelle Flores | Diane Hale | Marcella Johnson | Jacqueline Maricelli |
| Jeanne Fogg | Peggy Hall | Eugenia Johnson | Wendy Marici |
| Marilyn Forbes | Diane Hall | Sue Jones | Kate Marici |
| Katie Ford | Sarah Hammack | Carolyn Jones | Marisol Martinez |
| Mindy Foree | LeAnn Hanks | Hannah Jones | Paula Martinez |
| Phyllis Foree | Dena Hanks | Pamela Jones | Jennifer Masters |
| Tammy Fort | Katherine Harder | Cathy Jones | Pam McArthur |
| Traci Fort | Ellen Harnage | Vicky Jones | Carolyn McCain |
| Sue Foshee | Lisa Harrington | Marla Jones | Carrie McCleery |
| Relda Freeman | Jessica Harris | Beth Keahey | Janice McClure |
| Becky French | Beverly Harrison | Jeanie Keahey | Cathy McCombs |
| Patricia Freyaldenhoven | Jan Hart | Susan Kello | Melissa McCormick |
| Pat Gafford | Jeanne Harvey | Virginia Keniston | Sheila McCormick |
| Yolanda Gallardo | Carol Haynes | Jennifer Kerr | Pamela McDonald |
| Peggy Galvan | Liz Hays | Linda Kimbrough | Brenda McDonald |
| Jacqueline Garcia | Cindy Heald | Donna King | Jane McDonald |
| Martha Garcia | Shonda Hector | Karen King | Laura McGee |
| Maria Del Carmen Garcia | Deirdre Hedrick | Lori Kluesner | Norma McPhail |
| Ana Garcia | Julie Heinlein | Jean Kolaski | Amy McWhirter |
| Yolanda Gardner | Marie Henry | Jean Komarck | Dagmar Meeh |
| Merik Gardner | Connie Higgins | Vivian Kuhn | LaDonna Messarra |
| Betty Garner | Denyse Hines | Barbara Kurek | Mandy Meyers |
| Jeanie Garren | Allison Hipps | Stephanie Lacombe | Lori Michalsky |
| Katrina Garrett | Cathy Hipps | Ellen LaLonde | Kathy Milford |
| Irma Garza | Doris Hoke | Barbara Lambert | Tammy Miller |
| Emily Gentiles | Linda Holmes | Heather Lampard | Elizabeth Miller |
| Penny George | Debra Holzbach | Katie Lanclos | Jeanie Miller |
| Ashley Gibson | Shary Horn | Lisa Lane | Lynda Mills |
| Jackie Gieptner | Bevin Horne | Katherine Lavergne | Brittany Mills |
| Renee Gold | Jenny Howard | Carrie Lee | Cherie Mills |

# Acknowledgments (CONTINUED)

Wilma Mitchell
Alice Molina
Rachel Montemayor
Cynthia Montemayor-Allen
Cindy Mooney
Verna Moore
Meagen Moreno
Shari Morris
Betty Moss
Mary Muguerza
Sunnie Muguerza
Paula Munroe
Brenda Murphy
Jan Myers
Mica Nagle
LouAnn Nassif
Ashley Naylor
Carol Neel
Linda Nelson
Marta Nelson
Dana Nesmith
Carolyn Newton
Crystal Nicholson
Kyrbi Nighswonger
Georjean Nixon
Kristal Nutt
Eileen Oberman
Josie Oghomi
Angela Okafor
Gloria Olivarez
Elaine Olivarez
Kristi Ortiz
Celia Ortiz-Izaguirre
Chris Owens
Debbie Owens
Liliana Pando
Jennifer Pantoja
Patti Parker
Marsha Parrish
Donna Patrick
Sonia Patterson
Roxie Patterson
Jeanne Pearl
Sarah Pendergrass
Lillian Pendleton

Susan Peppers
Melissa Perez
Grace Perez
Sheila Petek
Laurie Petek
Katie Peterkoski
Sherry Peterson
Tammy Pierce
Monica Pike
Ramona Pipes
Martha Pitts
Marcia Polk
Tabatha Pond
Kaye Post
LaNell Pounds
Leah Pounds
Donna Powell
Kathy Purcell
Tonia Quackenbush
Yanet Quiceno
Pat Rabon
Wanda Rascoe
Sharon Reagan
Patricia Reeves
Ruth Reeves
Patti Reim
Ana Reyes
Margo Ricarte
Tracie Richeson
Cheryl Riggle
Sharon Rigsby
Lydia Riley
Julie Riley
Mary Rios-Celestina
Pamala Ritchie
Patti Roberts
Laura Roeder
Ruthie Rogers
Debbie Rosentiel
Debbie Rosentiel
Candy Ross
Ruth Rouse
Isabel Ruiz
Nancy Rumburg
Emily Ryan

Melisa Salazar
Lilia Sandoval
Gloria Saunders
Margaret Saunders
Becky Sayers
Cathy Schewe
Maureen Schneider
Lisa Schneider
Jessica Schwartz
Denise Serna
Joyce Shannon
Kathy Shatto
Mary Beth Shetz
Sandy Shiver
Gina Shoemaker
Cheryl Siens
Emily Siens
Christy Simmons
Kay Simpson
Pat Sims
Jan Smith
Stephanie Smith
Paulette Smith
Rebecca Smith
Sheryl Smith
Sandy Smith
Linda Smith
Denia Smith
Angelita Solis
Brittany Stanfield
Amber Steiner
Paula Stiles
Chitra Swamidoss
Sheila Tanksley
Lori Taylor
Neisha Teer
DeeDee Thompson
Erin Timmons
Bettie Tolar
Mary Trainer
Sarah Trammel
Lisa Trevino
Kay Tucker
Faye Tyler
Lisa Upshaw

Sarah Van Eenenoom
Linda Vasquez
Wanda Veltman
Susan Venier
Sylvia Verkerk
Rebekah Villano
Betzy Villarreal
Donna Vogel
Dora Waguespack
Leah Walker
Lucy Walker
Stephanie Walker
Mary Kay Wallace
Leah Walter
Shawnna Watts
Sherry Weaver
Jan Weede
Rosemarie Welch
Christina Weldon
Kim Wells
Mollie Whistler
Lori White
Ann White
Sarah Whitlock
Judy Wiggins
Betsy Wilbanks
Haylie Wilkerson
Beth Williams
Karen Williams
Persephone Williams
Misty Williston
Carol Wilson
Lorene Wirth
Kimberly Woitena
Jean Womack
Linda Wright
Suzanne Wright
Kristi Wright
Carol Wroten
Michele Zaunbrecher
Lorena Zavala
Brenda Zertuche
Diane Zimmerman

# About the Study

This Bible study is a simple tool to help you discover life-changing truths from God's Word. Think of this workbook as a chisel and your Bible as a gold mine. Each day you'll "dig-in" to God's Word to discover precious treasures that will enrich your life for His glory (Psalm 19:9-10, 119:162). Homework for this study will require approximately 30 minutes per day, five days per week.

A good translation of the Bible will be essential as you use this study. The *New Living Translation*, Second Edition, the *New International Version*, the *New American Standard Bible*, the *New King James Version*, or the *King James Version* are all very accurate translations and are highly recommended. In this study, the author will primarily use the *New Living Translation*.

# About the Author

Laurie Cole is the Founder and President of Priority Ministries, a ministry dedicated to encouraging and equipping women to love God most and seek Him first. Raised in a strong Christian home, Laurie became a Christian at an early age. But in her early twenties, God tested and taught her the importance of truly giving Him priority in her life.

In 1985, Laurie enrolled in an in-depth women's Bible study. Encouraged by the older women who led the study, Laurie received training and began teaching and leading a group where God affirmed His call upon her life to teach. For over 25 years, Laurie has taught dozens of Bible studies, spoken at numerous women's events and conferences, and is the author of five other Bible studies: *There Is a Season, The Temple, Beauty by The Book, Beauty by The Book for Teens,* and *Warrior Princess.* Her passion for God and hunger for His Word continues to grow.

A minister's wife, Laurie and her husband, Bill, serve the Lord at Sagemont Church in Houston, Texas, where he is the Associate Pastor of Worship and Praise. They have been married for 37 years and have three sons (David, Kevin, and J.J.), two beloved daughters-in-law (Stephanie and Rachael), and three glorious grandchildren (Ezra, Juliette, and Caroline).

# Table of Contents

are you a DISCIPLE?

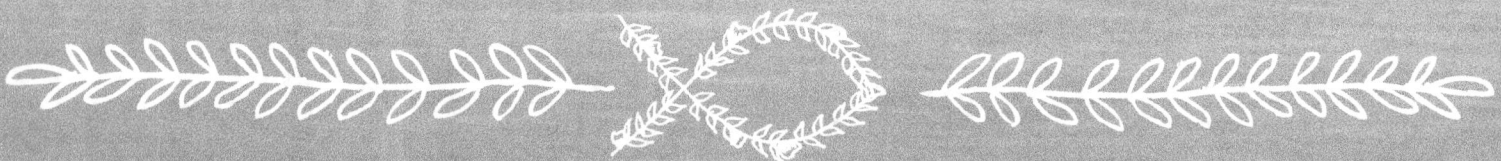

# Are you a Disciple: Goal & Purpose

## 3 Groups & 3 Goals

**Group 1:** Those of you who _____ _____.

**Goal:** That you will become a _____ who _____ _____.


**Group 2:** Those of you who are on your way to _____ _____.

**Goal:** That you will choose to _____ _____ no matter _____ _____.


**Group 3:** Those of you who will have the opportunity to become a _____ and a _____.

**Goal:** That you will choose to become a _____ and a _____.


## _____: A Role Model for All 3 Groups


1. She chose to _____ a _____. *Acts 18:1-3*


2. She chose to _____ a _____. *Acts 18:4-6, 18-19*


3. She was a _____ who _____ _____. *Acts 18:24-26, Romans 16:3-5*


*2 Timothy 4:19*

# week 1

## BACK STORIES & YOUR STORY

*If we answer the call to discipleship, where will it lead us? What decisions and partings will it demand? To answer this question we shall have to go to [Christ], for only he knows the answer. Only Jesus Christ, who bids us follow him knows the journey's end. But we do know that it will be a road of boundless mercy. Discipleship means joy.*

—Deitrich Bonhoeffer, *The Cost of Discipleship*[1]

# MY BACK STORY:

I became a Christian when I was just a child. Long before I could ever read or write, my parents taught me about God, Jesus, sin, salvation, and a whole host of Bible stories and songs. Secure in God's love and theirs, I placed my faith in Christ at the tender age of six.

I became a disciple when I was in my twenties. My marriage was unraveling. My world was falling apart. But in the great, big middle of that very insecure season, God drove me to my knees and drew me to Himself. And that's when I became a disciple.

What you've just read is my spiritual back story—a synopsis of my 50-year relationship with God.

Are you a Christian? If so, then are you a disciple? And if, perhaps, you're a little uncertain about what that second question means or how to answer it, don't worry. This week's homework will help you.

Please do not think, however, that I have forgotten about the first question: Are you a Christian? That, too, will be a very important part of this week's lesson because:

**You cannot be a disciple until you first become a Christian.**

And take it from someone whose world almost fell apart, Jesus wants you to be *both*.

# *day 1:* JESUS' BACK STORY

"In the beginning." Two books of the Bible (Genesis and the Gospel of John) begin with those three words.

Genesis reveals the beginning—the back story—of creation, the world, and mankind, but John's Gospel takes us even further back. It opens the curtain to eternity past and allows us to see the beginning—the back story—of the Word, Jesus Christ.

John's Gospel also reveals the back stories of Jesus' disciples. And if this were the first draft of this week's homework, I'd be introducing them to you right about now. But I never had peace about that first draft (or the second or even the third). Now I know why.

The first and foremost person you need to meet on this very first day of the very first week of your study isn't the disciples. It's the One the disciples followed: Jesus.

So, pick up your Bible and prepare to be awestruck as we begin "in the beginning."

1. Discover the divine back story of Jesus Christ by reading John 1:1-18. If this passage is familiar territory for you, I beg you not to rush through it. Take your time. Take it in.

   **NOTE:** The "Word" in this passage is Jesus.

### John 1:1-18

1 *In the beginning the Word already existed. The Word was with God, and the Word was God.*
2 *He existed in the beginning with God.*
3 *God created everything through him, and nothing was created except through him.*
4 *The Word gave life to everything that was created, and his life brought light to everyone.*
5 *The light shines in the darkness, and the darkness can never extinguish it.*
6 *God sent a man, John the Baptist,*
7 *to tell about the light so that everyone might believe because of his testimony.*
8 *John himself was not the light; he was simply a witness to tell about the light.*
9 *The one who is the true light, who gives light to everyone, was coming into the world.*
10 *He came into the very world he created, but the world didn't recognize him.*
11 *He came to his own people, and even they rejected him.*
12 *But to all who believed him and accepted him, he gave the right to become children of God.*
13 *They are reborn—not with a physical birth resulting from human passion or plan, but a birth that comes from God.*
14 *So the Word became human and made his home among us. He was full of unfailing love and faithfulness. And we have seen his glory, the glory of the Father's one and only Son.*
15 *John testified about him when he shouted to the crowds, "This is the one I was talking about when I said, 'Someone is coming after me who is far greater than I am, for he existed long before me.'"*
16 *From his abundance we have all received one gracious blessing after another.*
17 *For the law was given through Moses, but God's unfailing love and faithfulness came through Jesus Christ.*
18 *No one has ever seen God. But the one and only Son is himself God and is near to the Father's heart. He has revealed God to us.*

2.  Using words from the text as much as possible, answer the following questions about Jesus'
    back story:

    a.  When did Jesus' back story begin (v. 1)?

    b.  What did you learn about Jesus' history and relationship to God (vs. 1-3)?

    c.  How did Jesus affect everything and everyone including the darkness (vs. 4-5)?

    d.  What happened to Jesus, and how did others respond to Him (vs. 9-12, 14a)?

    e.  How are Jesus and God alike (vs. 14b, 17-18)?

    f.  How are Jesus and God different (vs. 14, 18)?

3.  As you read earlier, both Genesis and John start with the same three words: "in the beginning." But
    their similarities don't end there. Discover how Genesis reinforces and expands our understanding of
    God by studying a few key passages:

    a.  Read Genesis 1:1-2 and explain how it reinforces John 1:1-5.

b.  John 1 reveals that Jesus was with God in the beginning. But according to Genesis 1:2, who else was there?

c.  Read Genesis 1:26 and explain who "us" specifically is.

4.  All throughout history, countless individuals (including Mohammed, Buddha, L. Ron Hubbard, etc.) have established countless religions (including Islam, Buddhism, Scientology, etc.). According to what you've studied today, what makes Jesus and Christianity unique from them all?

When Jesus came into the world, three different groups of people responded to Him in three distinct ways:

1)  The world who didn't recognize Him (v. 10).

2)  The Jews (His people) who rejected Him (v. 11).

3)  The children of God who believed and accepted Him (v. 12).

These same three groups and responses remain true even today. But by believing the gospel of Jesus Christ, we can be part of that third group—the children of God.

So, what exactly is "the gospel"? The Apostle Paul calls it the "Good News," and he defines it in 1 Corinthians 15:1-4:

> *Let me now remind you, dear brothers and sisters, of the Good News…that saves you… [that] Christ died for our sins, just as the Scriptures said. He was buried, and he was raised from the dead on the third day, just as the Scriptures said.*
>
> —1 Corinthians 15:1-4

Very simply, the gospel is the Good News that Jesus died for our sins, was buried in the tomb, and rose from the dead so that we, too, may receive salvation and eternal life through Him.

The Apostle John described God's purpose in sending Jesus in the most well-known scripture of all time:

> *"For God loved the world so much that he gave his one and only Son, so that everyone who believes in him will not perish but have eternal life."*
>
> —John 3:16

Believing in Jesus means that we trust, commit, and place our faith in Him. In John 1:12, "believe" is used alongside the word "accept" (or "receive" in many translations). Believing in Jesus and receiving salvation go hand-in-hand. By placing our faith in Jesus, we receive salvation and the forgiveness of our sins.

Remember the question that I said I would not forget? It is The Most Important Question of this entire study, and now it's time for you to answer it: ***Are you a Christian?***

5.  Please answer that question by checking one of the following boxes:

☐ Yes, I am a Christian. I placed my faith in Jesus some time ago, and I have already taken the first essential step to become a disciple.

☐ Yes, today I am placing my faith in Jesus and receiving the gift of salvation. By becoming a Christian, I am also taking the first essential step to become a disciple.

☐ No, I cannot say that I am ready to place my faith in Christ and become a Christian today. But I do want to know more, and I will continue this study with an open heart.

*reflect*

6.  You've just spent the very first day of the very first week of this study in the very best way possible by getting to know Jesus (perhaps, for the very first time). Communicate with Him now by completing this one-sentence prayer:

*Dear Jesus, in a world where most people still don't recognize you for who you really are, thank you for showing me today that...*

_____

_____

_____

# *day 2:* BACK STORIES OF THE FIRST DISCIPLES: PART 1

Hello, my name is Laurie and I'm nosy.

For instance, when I'm having lunch with someone I don't know very well, I put on my "Oprah hat" (discreetly, of course) and interview them. I want to hear their story. I want to know what makes them tick. I want to learn about them and from them. My goal is to leave that lunch with a deeper understanding of who they really, *really* are. So should you ever find yourself across a table from me, consider yourself warned.

Today, I want you to get to know Jesus' very first disciples. You may already be familiar with some or all of them, but please approach today's study as if your knowledge of them is nil. Your goal: to conclude today's lesson with a deeper understanding of who the disciples really, *really* were. Enjoy a nice, nosy day in God's Word.

1.  Discover the back stories of Jesus' first disciples by reading John 1:15-51.

    **NOTE:** In this passage, John refers to John the Baptist. He was the forerunner of Jesus who announced Jesus' coming (John 1:6-8, 23). But John the Baptist is not the author of The Gospel of John. The author of this book is John, the disciple of Jesus, the son of Zebedee, also known as "the disciple whom Jesus loved" (John 21:20-25). He also authored 1st, 2nd, and 3rd John and The Revelation.

    ### John 1:15-51

    ¹⁵ *John testified about him when he shouted to the crowds, "This is the one I was talking about when I said, 'Someone is coming after me who is far greater than I am, for he existed long before me.'"*

    ¹⁶ *From his abundance we have all received one gracious blessing after another.*

    ¹⁷ *For the law was given through Moses, but God's unfailing love and faithfulness came through Jesus Christ.*

    ¹⁸ *No one has ever seen God. But the one and only Son is himself God and is near to the Father's heart. He has revealed God to us.*

    ¹⁹ *This was John's testimony when the Jewish leaders sent priests and Temple assistants from Jerusalem to ask John, "Who are you?"*

    ²⁰ *He came right out and said, "I am not the Messiah."*

    ²¹ *"Well then, who are you?" they asked. "Are you Elijah?" "No," he replied. "Are you the Prophet we are expecting?" "No."*

    ²² *"Then who are you? We need an answer for those who sent us. What do you have to say about yourself?"*

    —*continued next page*

## John 1:15-51 *(continued)*

<sup>23</sup> *John replied in the words of the prophet Isaiah: "I am a voice shouting in the wilderness, 'Clear the way for the LORD's coming!'"*

<sup>24</sup> *Then the Pharisees who had been sent*

<sup>25</sup> *asked him, "If you aren't the Messiah or Elijah or the Prophet, what right do you have to baptize?"*

<sup>26</sup> *John told them, "I baptize with water, but right here in the crowd is someone you do not recognize.*

<sup>27</sup> *Though his ministry follows mine, I'm not even worthy to be his slave and untie the straps of his sandal."*

<sup>28</sup> *This encounter took place in Bethany, an area east of the Jordan River, where John was baptizing.*

<sup>29</sup> *The next day John saw Jesus coming toward him and said, "Look! The Lamb of God who takes away the sin of the world!*

<sup>30</sup> *He is the one I was talking about when I said, 'A man is coming after me who is far greater than I am, for he existed long before me.'*

<sup>31</sup> *I did not recognize him as the Messiah, but I have been baptizing with water so that he might be revealed to Israel."*

<sup>32</sup> *Then John testified, "I saw the Holy Spirit descending like a dove from heaven and resting upon him.*

<sup>33</sup> *I didn't know he was the one, but when God sent me to baptize with water, he told me, 'The one on whom you see the Spirit descend and rest is the one who will baptize with the Holy Spirit.'*

<sup>34</sup> *I saw this happen to Jesus, so I testify that he is the Chosen One of God."*

<sup>35</sup> *The following day John was again standing with two of his disciples.*

<sup>36</sup> *As Jesus walked by, John looked at him and declared, "Look! There is the Lamb of God!"*

<sup>37</sup> *When John's two disciples heard this, they followed Jesus.*

<sup>38</sup> *Jesus looked around and saw them following. "What do you want?" he asked them. They replied, "Rabbi" (which means "Teacher"), "where are you staying?"*

<sup>39</sup> *"Come and see," he said. It was about four o'clock in the afternoon when they went with him to the place where he was staying, and they remained with him the rest of the day.*

<sup>40</sup> *Andrew, Simon Peter's brother, was one of these men who heard what John said and then followed Jesus.*

<sup>41</sup> *Andrew went to find his brother, Simon, and told him, "We have found the Messiah" (which means "Christ").*

<sup>42</sup> *Then Andrew brought Simon to meet Jesus. Looking intently at Simon, Jesus said, "Your name is Simon, son of John—but you will be called Cephas" (which means "Peter").*

<sup>43</sup> *The next day Jesus decided to go to Galilee. He found Philip and said to him, "Come, follow me."*

<sup>44</sup> *Philip was from Bethsaida, Andrew and Peter's hometown.*

<sup>45</sup> *Philip went to look for Nathanael and told him, "We have found the very person Moses and the prophets wrote about! His name is Jesus, the son of Joseph from Nazareth."*

<sup>46</sup> *"Nazareth!" exclaimed Nathanael. "Can anything good come from Nazareth?" "Come and see for yourself," Philip replied.*

<sup>47</sup> *As they approached, Jesus said, "Now here is a genuine son of Israel—a man of complete integrity."*

<sup>48</sup> *"How do you know about me?" Nathanael asked. Jesus replied, "I could see you under the fig tree before Philip found you."*

*—continued next page*

⁴⁹ "Then Nathanael exclaimed, "Rabbi, you are the Son of God—the King of Israel!"

⁵⁰ Jesus asked him, "Do you believe this just because I told you I had seen you under the fig tree? You will see greater things than this."

⁵¹ Then he said, "I tell you the truth, you will all see heaven open and the angels of God going up and down on the Son of Man, the one who is the stairway between heaven and earth."

2. How did the very first disciples meet Jesus?

3. Before becoming disciples of Jesus, who did some of the disciples follow (v. 35), and what does this reveal about them spiritually?

4. Before meeting Jesus, what did the first disciples already know about Him? Read the following passages, and record what John the Baptist would have already taught them about Jesus. Also, please take time to read a few verses before and after each passage to enhance your understanding of the context.

   a. John 1:15-18

   b. John 1:26-27

   c. John 1:29

   d. John 1:30-36

5.  You just read John's account of the baptism of Christ (John 1:31-34). It is important to note that all four of The Gospels—Matthew, Mark, Luke, and John—include the story of Jesus' baptism. Discover the significance of baptism and get to know the disciples a little more by reading Luke 3:3 and answering the questions that follow.

    *Then John went from place to place on both sides of the Jordan River,*
    *preaching that people should be baptized to show that they had turned to God*
    *to receive forgiveness for their sins.*

    —Luke 3.3

    a.  What did John the Baptist teach about baptism and its significance?

    b.  Think about this: would John's disciples have been baptized?
        Circle your answer.

        Yes        No        I'm not sure

    c.  Explain your answer to question "b."

    d.  Why was Jesus, the sinless Son of God, baptized? What did His baptism reveal and prove? Review John 1:31-34 to answer this question.

Let's pause for a few paragraphs to ponder Jesus' baptism.

Before He began His public ministry, before a single disciple ever followed Him, before preaching His first sermon or performing His first miracle, Jesus was baptized. The same One who was "in the beginning…with God…and…[who] was God" (John 1:1 NASB) left His hometown of Nazareth one day and set out for the Jordan River to be baptized by John.

The baptism of Christ reveals a beautiful principle to every potential disciple: baptism was a priority to Jesus—even over ministry and service to others. Therefore, if you desire to follow Christ and be His disciple, you should also follow Him in baptism. And the sooner the better. His priorities should be your priorities.

One final point about baptism: salvation is essential for baptism, but baptism is not essential for salvation. The best example of this would be the thief who received salvation as he hung on the cross next to Jesus and to whom Jesus promised, "I assure you, today you will be with me in paradise" (Luke 23:43). That thief, however, did not have the opportunity to be baptized. We do.

6. Who were Jesus' first disciples? What were their names, and what common ties did they share (John 1:35-47)?

**NOTE:** Many theologians believe the unnamed disciple in this passage is John, the author of this book (not John the Baptist).

7. Read the following verses, and record how the first disciples described Jesus:

   a. John 1:38: _____

   b. John 1:41: _____

   c. John 1:45: _____

   d. John 1:49: _____

Did you notice the chain reaction in John 1:35-51? It begins when John the Baptist directs two of his disciples to follow Jesus. It continues when one of those men finds his brother and brings Him to Christ. Then Jesus reaches out to Philip and invites him to, "Follow Me" (John 1:43). The chain reaction concludes as Philip finds Nathanael and brings him to Christ.

These five men—Andrew, John, Simon Peter, Philip, and Nathanael—were the very first disciples. The chain reaction that led them to Christ continues today. And you are part of it.

8. As you reflect upon your own life, who did God use to direct and bring you to Jesus? Even more importantly, who does God want you to bring to Christ? Write these names in the space provided. Conclude your time of reflection by thanking God for those He used to bring you to Christ and by praying for those He wants you to reach.

_____

_____

_____

_____

# *day 3:* WHY FOLLOW JESUS?

The title of this study is actually a question: Are you a disciple? Answering that question is one of the primary objectives of this study. But that is not the question you will be dealing with today. This is:

**Why do you want to become a disciple of Jesus?**

It's a nosy question, and it strikes at the very heart of our motives for following Christ. But nosy me isn't the one who is asking. Jesus is. In fact, the very first recorded words of Christ in John's Gospel are, basically, that very question:

*Jesus looked around and saw them following. "What do you want?" he asked them.*

—John 1:38

Jesus wanted those first disciples to tell Him why they were following Him. But the disciples ducked His question with a question of their own: "Where are you staying?" (John 1:38). Without prodding or pressing them to answer His question, Jesus simply replied, "Come and see" (John 1:39).

Why did Jesus ask such a blunt, pointed question in the first place? After all, He already knew everything within their hearts including every word they were about to speak (Luke 9:47). So why did He even ask? And for that matter, why does He ever ask us anything?

He asks because we need to answer. He asks because we need to examine our hearts and motives. He asks because He wants us to confess what we too often suppress. And above all, He asks because He longs to lavish His love, mercy, and grace upon us.

Why do you want to become a disciple? Why follow Jesus? Allow Jesus to show you the answers to those questions for Himself today. All you need to do is "come and see" (John 1:39).

1. Yesterday you met Nathanael. Review his first encounter with Christ by reading John 1:47-51 and answering the questions that follow:

### John 1:47-51

47 *As they approached, Jesus said, "Now here is a genuine son of Israel—a man of complete integrity."*

48 *"How do you know about me?" Nathanael asked. Jesus replied, "I could see you under the fig tree before Philip found you."*

49 *Then Nathanael exclaimed, "Rabbi, you are the Son of God—the King of Israel!"*

50 *Jesus asked him, "Do you believe this just because I told you I had seen you under the fig tree? You will see greater things than this."*

51 *Then he said, "I tell you the truth, you will all see heaven open and the angels of God going up and down on the Son of Man, the one who is the stairway between heaven and earth."*

a. What question did Jesus ask, and what promises did He make to Nathanael (v. 50-51)?

Question (v. 50a):

Promise # 1 (v. 50b):

Promise # 2 (v. 51):

b. How did Jesus describe Himself to Nathanael? Fill in the blanks:

"The Son of Man, the one who is the _____ between
_____ and _____."

2. Three years after His first encounter with Nathanael, Jesus met with His disciples for a final supper and prepared them for His arrest and crucifixion. Read this account from John 14:1-6 using your own Bible, then answer the following questions:

a. What did Jesus say the disciples already knew (v. 4)?

"You know _____ _____ to where I am going."

b. How did Thomas respond to Jesus? What question did he ask (v. 5b)?

"How can we know _____ _____?"

c. How did Jesus answer Thomas (v. 6a)?

"I am _____ _____."

d. In Acts 1:9-10, Jesus fulfilled His promises to both Nathanael (John 1:50) and Thomas (John 14:6). Read Acts 1:9-10, and desribe how He did it.

e. According to John 1:51, John 14:6, and Acts 1:9-10, why follow Jesus?

3. The small band of disciples had only been following Jesus for three days when they witnessed something very significant. Discover what it was by reading John 2:1-11, then answer the questions that follow:

a. What did the disciples see Jesus do firsthand?

b. What was the significance of what Jesus did (v. 11)?

c. How did it affect the disciples (v. 11)?

d. According to John 1, the disciples already believed Jesus was the Messiah and the Son of God. So, what happened to their new-found faith in Christ in John 2:11?

4. Jesus' first miracle led to many, many others. "Come and see" (John 1:39) a few more. Read the following passages and describe briefly the miracles Jesus performed:

   a. Luke 8:22-25

   b. Luke 8:26-37

   c. Luke 8:40-56

5. According to the passages you've just studied in Questions 3 and 4, why follow Jesus?

6. Jesus was the fulfillment of the Old Testament prophecies and promises of the Messiah. "Come and see" (John 1:39) some of them by reading the following passages and recording a brief description of how Jesus fulfilled Old Testament prophecy:

   **NOTE:** In some (but not all) Bible translations, scriptures from the Old Testament *may* be capitalized or indented when they are quoted in the New Testament.

   a. Matthew 11:1-6 / Isaiah 35:4-6, 61:1

   b. Matthew 13:33-35 / Psalm 78:2

   c. Matthew 21:1-5 / Zechariah 9:9

   d. Matthew 27:34-50 / Psalm 22:6-8, 11-18 (Keep in mind that Psalm 22 was written hundreds of years before Christ came and hundreds of years before crucifixions ever took place.)

7. According to the passages you've just studied in Question 6, why follow Jesus?

*reflect*

8. What have you seen Jesus do in your own life? Describe one or two of the most significant ways He has proven to you that He is "the way, the truth and the life" (John 14:6).

_____

_____

_____

_____

_____

_____

_____

# *day* 4: BACK STORIES OF THE FIRST DISCIPLES: PART 2

How did the disciples become disciples? That's the #1 Question nosy me wanted to know before I started writing this study. Who were they, and what were they like before they became the Apostles—the pillars and leaders of the Christian faith?

Today, as you continue studying the back stories of the disciples, my hope is that you will not only gain a deeper understanding of who they were, but that you will also see how much you have in common.

P.S. Yesterday's homework was longer than usual, so today's will be shorter. (You're welcome.)

1. You met Jesus' first disciples in John 1-2. After following Jesus to Jerusalem, Judea, and Samaria (John 2:13-17, 3:22, 4:1-8), the disciples returned to their hometown near the Sea of Galilee, and Jesus went to Nazareth, His hometown (Luke 4).

   The reunion between Jesus, Peter, Andrew, James, and John is recorded in the following passages. Read each passage, then record:

   - The key details of their reunion.
   - Jesus' call and their responses.
   - Your own personal and spiritual insights.

   **NOTE:** You will notice that these three accounts are somewhat different. However, most scholars believe they are parallel accounts of the same story as told by three different men with three different perspectives.

   a. Matthew 4:18-22

   b. Mark 1:16-20

   c. Luke 5:1-11

2.  Conclude your homework today by answering a few key questions about the account you just read from Luke 5.

    a.  What were the results of Peter's first fishing trip (v. 5)?

    b.  How did Peter address Jesus prior to his second fishing trip (v. 5)?

    c.  What did Peter do and confess after the second fishing trip (v. 8)?

    d.  How did Peter address Jesus after the second fishing trip (v. 8), and how does this differ from the way he previously addressed Jesus in verse 5?

    e.  How did Jesus reply to Peter's confession, and what does this reveal about Jesus (v. 10)?

*reflect*

3.  Have you had a Luke 5:8 experience recently? Describe it (briefly) in the space below. If you haven't confessed it to Jesus yet, do that now. Finally, write a one or two sentence prayer of thanksgiving to Jesus, the One who forgives sinners and gives them a future and a hope.

    _____

    _____

    _____

    _____

# *day 5*: BACK STORIES OF THE FIRST DISCIPLES: PART 3

You have already met five of the disciples, and today you will meet the remaining seven. But these twelve men weren't the only disciples. There were many others, many of whom were women! (We have Luke to thank for providing us with some wonderful details about them.)

As you complete today's study, there are three questions you need to consider:

1) Who did Jesus call to become His disciple?

2) Who does Jesus call to become His disciple today?

And, of course:

3) Are you a disciple?

Enjoy some sweet time in God's Word!

1. Read Luke 5:27-32 and meet the disciple "Levi", aka "Matthew." Then answer the questions that follow.

**Luke 5:27-32**

²⁷ *Later, as Jesus left the town, he saw a tax collector named Levi sitting at his tax collector's booth. "Follow me and be my disciple," Jesus said to him.*

²⁸ *So Levi got up, left everything, and followed him.*

²⁹ *Later, Levi held a banquet in his home with Jesus as the guest of honor. Many of Levi's fellow tax collectors and other guests also ate with them.*

³⁰ *But the Pharisees and their teachers of religious law complained bitterly to Jesus' disciples, "Why do you eat and drink with such scum?"*

³¹ *Jesus answered them, "Healthy people don't need a doctor—sick people do.*

³² *I have come to call not those who think they are righteous, but those who know they are sinners and need to repent."*

a. How is Matthew unique from the other disciples you have studied thus far? Describe how he is different from Peter and his companions.

are you a DISCIPLE?

b.  How is Matthew like the other disciples? Describe what he has in common with Peter and his companions.

c.  What does Luke 5:29 reveal about Matthew?

In my own study of Matthew, I learned something about him that I'd never really noticed before: not one single word of anything he ever said is recorded in the Scriptures. This makes me think that he probably wasn't much of a talker.

Matthew was, however, a keen listener and observer. He wrote the Gospel of Matthew, and none of the other Gospels include more of Jesus' teachings and sermons than his does.[2] Matthew also had a very broad knowledge of the Old Testament quoting it over 50 times and referring to it over 75 times in his Gospel.[3]

One more thing about Matthew: all throughout his Gospel, he refers to himself as "Matthew the tax collector." None of the other Gospels refer to him in that way.[4] Personally, I think that's because Matthew never got over the two most gracious words a tax collector like him ever heard: Follow Me.

2.  According to Luke 5:32, who does Jesus call, and what do every Christian and disciple have in common?

3.  Read Luke 6:13-16 and record a complete list of the names of the 12 disciples.

1) _____     2) _____     3) _____

4) _____     5) _____     6) _____

7) _____     8) _____     9) _____

10) _____    11) _____    12) _____

4. What other title/position did Jesus give to these men (v. 13)? _____

After appointing the 12 disciples, Luke 6:17 records that "Jesus came down [the mountain] with them and stood on a level place; and there was a large crowd of His disciples, and a great throng of people" (NASB). This passage reveals that Jesus had many disciples. The 12 were set apart as apostles, but all who followed Christ during that time were called "disciples."

**NOTE:** You may notice that Nathanael's name is missing from this list. Many Bible scholars believe that Nathanael and Bartholomew are the same person.

5. Meet some of my favorite disciples by reading the following passage:

### Luke 8:1-3

¹ *Soon afterward Jesus began a tour of the nearby towns and villages, preaching and announcing the Good News about the Kingdom of God. He took his twelve disciples with him,*

² *along with some women he had healed and from whom he had cast out evil spirits. Among them were Mary Magdalene, from whom he had cast out seven demons;*

³ *Joanna, the wife of Chuza, Herod's business manager; Susanna; and many others who were contributing their own resources to support Jesus and his disciples.*

Circle the names and pronouns of the women who followed Jesus, and notice what He did for them. What did they do for Jesus?

6. Another group of female disciples is mentioned in Mark 15:40-41. Read that passage—and be sure to note the context—then answer the following questions:

   a. Who are these women and, according to this passage, where are they?

   b. What does this reveal about them and their relationship to Jesus?

   c. Describe their relationship to Jesus prior to this event (v. 41).

*reflect*

7. You've just studied the back stories of Matthew and several women who followed Christ. What about your back story? Where were you, what were you doing, and what were you like when you met Jesus?

_____

_____

_____

_____

_____

_____

_____

_____

_____

8. As you conclude your first week of study, I have one final question for you: Are you a disciple? Circle your answer.

Yes          No

*Today we have substituted creedal belief for personal belief, and that is why so many are devoted to causes and so few devoted to Jesus Christ. People do not want to be devoted to Jesus, but only to the cause He started… If I am devoted to the cause of humanity only, I will soon be exhausted and come to the place where my love will falter; but if I love Jesus Christ personally and passionately, I can serve humanity though men treat me as a door-mat. The secret of a disciple's life is devotion to Jesus Christ… It is like a corn of wheat, which falls into the ground and dies, but presently it will spring up and alter the whole landscape (John 12:24).*

—Oswald Chambers, *My Utmost for His Highest*[5]

are you a DISCIPLE?

# The Call of Christ

**To Salvation:** _____ *John 1:12*

    **Question:** Why should you _____ in Jesus?

    1.   Because He is _____. *John 1:1-2*

    2.   Because He is _____/_____. *John 1:1, 8:24*

    3.   Because His _____ _____ that He is God's Son. *John 2:7-9*

    4.   Because He _____ the Old Testament _____. *Ps. 22, John 2:17*

    5.   Because He is the _____ _____ to God. *John 14:6, Rom 1:16*

**To Discipleship:** _____ _____ *John 1:43*

    **Question:** Why should you _____ _____?

    1.   Because He will instruct and enable you to _____ _____ you've _____ _____ before. *Luke 5:4-5*

    2.   Because He will allow you to _____ and _____ things you've never _____ or _____ before. *Luke 5:6-7*

    3.   Because He will keep you _____ and keenly aware of your own _____. *Luke 5:8, James 4:6*

    4.   Because He will _____ and _____ you unconditionally. *Luke 5:10*

    5.   Because He has an eternal _____ and _____ for your life. *Luke 5:10-11*

        ***You've seen why you should accept the call of Christ.***

        ***Now the only question is:*** _____ _____?

are you a DISCIPLE?

# week 2

# CASUAL CHRISTIANS vs. DEVOTED DISCIPLES

*It is not without significance that the word "disciple" occurs in the New Testament 269 times, "Christian" only 3 times, and "believers" 2 times. This surely indicates that the task of the church is not so much to make "Christians" or "believers" but "disciples." A disciple must, of course, be a believer; but according to Christ's conditions of discipleship (Luke 14:25–33), not all believers are disciples of the New Testament stamp.*

— J. Oswald Sanders, *Spiritual Discipleship*[1]

# *day 1:* WHAT IS A DISCIPLE?

*Semper fidelis.* It is the Latin phrase for "always faithful," and it is best known as the motto of the United States Marine Corps. To be a Marine is to commit to be faithful to country, to the Corps, to the mission, and to every fellow Marine. Commitment to *semper fidelis* extends far beyond the term of active duty. *Semper fi* is a commitment for life.

When I think about what it means to be a disciple, I think of the Marines. I think of *semper fidelis*, and I also think of the phrase that defines their elite status: "the few and the proud."

This week, your homework will be a little like boot camp. It is designed to teach you the core values and requirements for being a disciple. And although I'm no drill instructor, I now proclaim without reservation my #1 goal for this week's homework: to prepare you to become part of the few and the ~~proud~~ faithful, the disciples.

1. Welcome to Boot Camp. Begin by learning the definition of "disciple." Read the following definitions, then compose your own personalized definition.

    a. *The Holman Illustrated Bible Dictionary* defines "disciple" as follows:

    > In the Greek world the word "disciple" normally referred to an adherent of a particular teacher or religious/philosophical school. It was the task of the disciple to learn, study, and pass along the sayings and teachings of the master. In rabbinic Judaism the term "disciple" referred to one who was committed to the interpretations of Scripture and religious tradition given him by the master or rabbi. Through a process of learning which would include a set meeting time and such pedagogical methods as question and answer, instruction, repetition, and memorization, the disciple would become increasingly devoted to the master and the master's teachings. In time, the disciple would likewise pass on the traditions to others.[2]

b. *The Complete Word Study Dictionary New Testament* defines "disciple" as follows:

> [The term "disciple"] means more in the New Testament than a mere pupil or learner. It is an adherent who accepts the instruction given to him and makes it his rule of conduct… Jesus had disciples in the sense that they believed and made His teaching the basis of their conduct.[3]

c. In his excellent book *Spiritual Discipleship*, J. Oswald Sanders says:

> The word *disciple* means "a learner," but Jesus infused into that simple word a wealth of profound meaning. As used by Him and by Paul, it means "a learner or pupil who accepts the teaching of Christ, not only in belief but also in lifestyle." This involves acceptance of the views and practice of the Teacher. In other words, it means learning with the purpose to obey what is learned. It involves a deliberate choice, a definite denial, and a determined obedience.[4]

d. Considering all that you've just read, compose your own personalized definition of *disciple* by completing the following sentence:

Becoming a disciple of Jesus means that I will _____

_____

_____.

2. To review what you just learned, take a quick open book test. Read the following statements, compare them with the definitions in Question 1, and circle whether they are true or false.

a. Becoming a disciple doesn't happen quickly. It is a process.

    True        False

b. As a disciple grows and becomes stronger, she will become increasingly independent from her teacher.

    True        False

c. After a disciple has received instruction and training, she will instruct and train others.

    True        False

d. A disciple doesn't just learn from her teacher; a disciple applies and practices what she learns.

    True        False

e. A mature disciple will eventually be able to pick and choose which tenets of her training to apply to her life.

    True        False

Jesus set very clear and very high standards for those who would be His disciples, and you are about to study them. But before you do, prepare for enemy attack. Because even as you are reading these words, heavy fire is heading your way. In an attempt to dissuade, discourage and ultimately defeat you from even thinking that someone like you could become a disciple, Satan will assault your mind with an unholy arsenal of fear, intimidation and doubt this week.

Stand firm, precious sister. Do not believe the propaganda that your past (or present) disqualifies you from discipleship. When the enemy does his best to convince you that the requirements for discipleship are too high for you to attain, do not retreat. Remember that even in the midst of the battle, Jesus invites you to, "Come, follow Me." Forward march.

3. What did Jesus teach about discipleship? What are the requirements? Read each passage on the following chart and record a list of the requirements for becoming a disciple:

   NOTE: For greater understanding and clarity, please read each passage from two or three different Bible translations such as the *New American Standard Bible*, *New Living Translation*, and the *Amplified Bible*. Feel free to use Bible apps or websites like **biblegateway.com**.

### The Requirements for Becoming a Disciple

Luke 9:22-26—*Jesus taught that a disciple must…*

Luke 14:25-33—*Jesus taught that a disciple must…*

4. The definition for *follow Me* is very similar to the definition for *disciple*. Read the following definitions, then complete the sentence:

   a. From *Practical Word Studies in The New Testament*:

   The word ["follow"] means to be a follower or companion; to be a disciple; to accompany; to come or go with. To follow has the idea of seeking to be in union with and in the likeness of. It is following Christ, seeking to be just like Him. Again, this is not a passive behavior, but an active commitment and walk. It is energy and effort, action and work. It is going after Christ with zeal and energy, struggling and seeking to follow in His footsteps, no matter the cost.[5]

   b. From *The Complete Word Study Dictionary New Testament*:

   The individual calling to follow Jesus involved abiding fellowship with Him… The first thing involved in following Jesus is a cleaving to Him in believing trust and obedience. Those cleaving to Him must also follow His leading and act according to His example (John 8:12; 10:4, 5, 27). Hence constant stress is laid by the Lord Jesus upon the need of self-denial and fellowship of the cross (Matt. 8:19, 12:26). Following Jesus thus denotes a fellowship of faith as well as a fellowship of life, sharing in His sufferings not only inwardly, but outwardly if necessary (Matt. 9:9, 19, 27). Such outward fellowship with Jesus, however, could not continue without inner moral and spiritual fellowship, without a life resembling His and a self-denying sharing of His cross.[6]

   Following Jesus means that I will _____

   _____

   _____

   _____

   _____.

5. Use your Bible to revisit the following passages from your study last week. Record how the disciples responded to Jesus' invitation (what they did) and how their response fulfilled the requirements for becoming a disciple.

   a. Matt. 4:19-20

   b. Mark 1:16-20

c.   Luke 5:10-11

At this point, you should have a good understanding of what it means to follow Jesus and be His disciple. Now it's time to take it to the next level—from your head to your heart—by applying what you've learned to your own life.

*reflect*

6.   Meditate on the requirements for becoming a disciple in Question 2. Is anything holding you back from becoming a disciple? What changes to your life and routine would be necessary for you to follow Jesus? Take these questions before the Lord in prayer. Record what God reveals to you and your response to Him.

God is showing me that _____

_____

_____

As a result, I am responding to Him by _____

_____

_____

## *day* 2: DISCIPLE WANNABES VS. THE REAL THING

When I came to Christ as a child, I didn't understand all that being a Christian really meant. And I certainly didn't know any of the truths and principles you studied yesterday.

But in my early twenties, I came to a spiritual crossroad where I was faced with two options:
1) I could stay on "Laurie Lane" and continue doing life my way with a little Jesus on the side, or
2) I could take the "Follow Me Road" and lose my life to find it.

Both options scared me. Option 1 was the familiar path that had led my life and marriage to brokenness and despair. Option 2 was unfamiliar and would require enormous change and, because I was so broken, I wasn't even sure if I could change.

Turns out, brokenness is a beautiful thing. When you finally reach the point of knowing you cannot, Jesus comes and says, "I can."

Today you will study the spiritual crossroad stories of five men. Each of them faced two options: 1) to remain where they were and continue to do life their way, or 2) to follow Jesus and do life His way.

Four out of five chose Option 1.

Are you at a spiritual crossroad? Precious sister, I implore and exhort you to choose Option 2. Be the one in five. Discover the beauty brokenness brings by losing your life to find it.

1. Luke 9 records the stories of three "Disciple Wannabes." Read their stories in the following passage keeping in mind that Jesus knew what was in each of their hearts. After you have finished reading the passage, answer the questions that follow.

   **NOTE:** There are two translations of Luke 9:59 to help you interpret that verse.

   ### Luke 9:57-62

   57 *As they were walking along, someone said to Jesus, "I will follow you wherever you go."*
   58 *But Jesus replied, "Foxes have dens to live in, and birds have nests, but the Son of Man has no place even to lay his head."*
   59 *He said to another person, "Come, follow me." The man agreed, but he said, "Lord, first let me return home and bury my father."*
   60 *But Jesus told him, "Let the spiritually dead bury their own dead! Your duty is to go and preach about the Kingdom of God."*
   61 *Another said, "Yes, Lord, I will follow you, but first let me say good-bye to my family."*
   62 *But Jesus told him, "Anyone who puts a hand to the plow and then looks back is not fit for the Kingdom of God."*

   ### Luke 9:59 (AMP)

   59 *And He said to another, Become My disciple, side with My party, and accompany Me! But he replied, Lord, permit me first to go and bury (await the death of) my father.*

   a. What does Jesus' response (v. 58) reveal about Disciple Wannabe #1?

b. What does Jesus' response (v. 60) reveal about Disciple Wannabe #2?

c. What does Jesus' response (v. 62) reveal about Disciple Wannabe #3?

d. What specific scriptural requirements disqualified these three Disciple Wannabes from becoming disciples? Use the chart you created in Day One, Question 3, to help answer this question.

2. Did you notice that two of the men in Luke 9 used the same phrase and excuse "but first"? When you sense that Jesus is calling you to say or do something, what are your top three favorite "but first" excuses?

#1:

#2:

#3:

3. In what specific issue or area of your life is Jesus calling you to put first things first?

4. Mark 10:17-23 records the story of Disciple Wannabe #4. Use your Bible to read this passage, and answer the following questions:

   a. What did this man want (v. 17)?

   b. What evidence reveals that he was sincere (v. 17)?

   c. What did Jesus say it would take for this Disciple Wannabe to follow Him?

   d. How did the man respond, and what does this reveal about his priorities?

   e. What specific scriptural requirements disqualified this Disciple Wannabe from becoming a disciple? Use the chart you created in Day One, Question 3, to help answer this question.

All four of the men you just met came face to face with Jesus and then turned away. At the crossroads, they chose Option 1, to do life their own way.

The Book of Acts records the story of the fifth and final man you will meet today. He also experienced a face-to-face encounter with Jesus. But unlike all four Disciple Wannabes, he chose Option 2, to follow Jesus. And what a difference this made in his life—and ultimately in ours as well!

Spend the rest of your study today with someone who is no Disciple Wannabe. He's the Real Thing, a true disciple of Jesus Christ: Paul.

**NOTE:** In the passages you are about to study, Paul is also known as Saul.

5.  Study Paul before, during, and after he came to the crossroad in his life. Read the passages in the chart below, and record your answers to the question in each section. Also, be sure to record any insights the Holy Spirit reveals to you as you study Paul.

| Paul Before the Crossroad | Paul at the Crossroad | Paul After the Crossroad |
|---|---|---|
| Acts 8:1-3, 9:1-2 - *Who was Paul and what was he like before the crossroad?* | Acts 9:3-9 - *What happened to Paul at the crossroad?* | Acts 9:10-30 - *How did Paul prove he was a true disciple?* |

*reflect*

6.  Are you at a spiritual crossroad? How is Jesus calling you to follow Him in this season of your life? Reflect on these questions, and record your answer.

_____

_____

_____

_____

# *day* 3: BLESSINGS & BENEFITS OF DISCIPLESHIP

You know it is frostbite weather when the driver of your airport shuttle arrives at the car rental lot, stops beside a row of assorted cars and says, "Folks, because of the extreme conditions, exit the shuttle quickly and pick any car you want. The keys are in the car. No agents are on duty to assist you. Just get in a car, drive to the gate attendant, give them your info, and you'll be on your way." Personally, I don't know how the good people of Chicago survive Chicago winters.

As lifelong Texans and lovers of mild winters, our family doesn't do snow and cold weather well. But on that bone-chilling January day, a Cole was graduating from Navy Boot Camp just outside Chicago, and we weren't about to allow a sub-zero wind chill factor to keep us from getting there.

When we finally arrived at the Navy compound, several hundred shivering cadets were standing at attention in groups outside the gym where the graduation was about to take place. One of those hypothermic cadets was Kevin, our second son. When he finally marched into the gym, his lips were blue and his face was pallid. But after persevering through eight long weeks of grueling training and excruciating weather, Kevin had made it through Boot Camp. And it was totally worth it.

Kevin's military service was brief—just a four-year stint. But the results of those four years continue to mark his life in a very positive way. And as his parents, we are very grateful for the lifelong benefits he will receive for serving his country.

Today, as you continue your Boot Camp experience, you will discover some of the blessings and benefits of being a disciple. Whether your service to the Lord has been brief or decades long, you are eligible to receive full benefits. Following Jesus. It is totally worth it.

1. Begin your study today by reading the passages in the chart below and recording your answers to the question in each section.

### The Blessings & Benefits of Following Jesus

| *Who receives them...* | *What will they receive...* |
|---|---|
| Matthew 19:27-30 | |
| Mark 10:28-31 | |
| John 8:12 | |
| John 10:4-5 | |
| John 10:27-29 | |
| John 12:26 | |

2. John 13-17 is known as "The Upper Room Discourse." It is the record of Jesus' final words to the disciples prior to His arrest and crucifixion. To prepare and encourage them for what they were about to face, Jesus shares some of the blessings and benefits they will soon receive. Read the passages in the chart below and record your answers to the question in each section as you did in Question 1.

### The Blessings & Benefits of Discipleship

| Who receives them... | What will they receive... |
| --- | --- |
| John 14:2-3 | |
| John 14:12 | |
| John 14:13-14 | |
| John 14:16-18, 26 | |
| John 14:27 | |
| John 15:11 | |

3. As you review and meditate upon the charts you just created, place a checkmark beside the blessings and benefits that have meant the most to you in your walk with Christ.

4. Which of these blessings and benefits do you most need in your life right now and why?

5. The final passage you will study today is one of my favorites: Philippians 3:7-14. It is written by Paul, whom you studied yesterday. Using your own Bible, read this passage and answer the questions that follow:

   a. How is this passage similar to the two passages you studied in Day 1, Question 3 (Luke 9:22-26 and Luke 14:25-33), and what parallel principles did you see Paul practice as a disciple?

   b. According to Philippians 3:7-14, what are the blessings and benefits of following Christ? What makes discipleship so worthwhile?

*reflect*

6. In order to press on in his ministry and relationship with Jesus, Paul said that he had to "focus on this one thing: Forgetting the past and looking forward to what lies ahead" (Phil. 3:13). Do you need to forget something in your own past in order to press on as a disciple of Jesus? It may be something good and positive or bad and negative. What's keeping you tied to the past and incapable of moving forward? Reflect on these questions, and record your answers on the lines below.

Finally, take any past issues or experiences that are preventing you from pressing on to the Lord in prayer. Leave them with Him and forget them. Commit today to press on.

**NOTE:** If your past includes abuse, abandonment, depression, or other forms of loss or trauma, I cannot encourage you enough to seek wise, professional, Christian counseling. There are times when we all need someone else to help us push through the past and point us to specific, scriptural paths for pressing on.

_____

_____

_____

## *day 4:* WHAT IS A CASUAL CHRISTIAN?

Yesterday you studied four Disciple Wannabes who, by all outward appearances, seemed so eager to become disciples. In fact, they were right on the brink of making the life-changing decision to do exactly what Peter, John, Andrew, Nathanael, Matthew, Paul and many others did: to forsake all to follow Christ.

But when it came right down to it, they did not.

Have you ever been so worked up spiritually that you told yourself something like this: "From this moment on, I'm going to be a better Christian than I've ever been before"? Maybe you heard a great sermon, attended a fantastic retreat, or were lifted to heaven's heights at a Christian concert or conference. And in all sincerity and eagerness, you came right to the brink of making a life-changing decision to forsake all to follow Christ.

But when it came right down to it, you did not.

If you answered yes, then you know what it means to be a Disciple Wannabe.

I've been a Disciple Wannabe. And I can tell you that the spiritual high that precedes it camouflages the spiritual low that is certain to follow. Truth is, every eager, enthusiastic Disciple Wannabe is just one decision away from becoming what I call a "Casual Christian." Been there, done that, too, and by God's grace alone, I can testify to the damage and dangers of Casual Christianity.

Today's lesson is critical, and you better believe that your enemy is going to do everything possible to encourage you to skip it. Trust me when I tell you that Casual Christianity is a killer. It can kill your marriage. It can kill your relationships. It can kill your career. It can kill your influence and effectiveness for Christ. In fact, I firmly believe that Casual Christianity is the #1 disciple killer in the church today.

Arm yourself, precious sister. Pick up your sword—your Bible—and prepare to do battle with the enemy and, perhaps, with yourself. Because as you study the definition of Casual Christianity, you may discover there are certain aspects in your own life where it defines you.

1. One of the best descriptions and illustrations of Casual Christianity is found in 1 Corinthians. Read the following passages, and record your answer to each question:

   a. 1 Cor. 1:2-5—How does Paul (the author of 1 Corinthians) describe the people of the church of Corinth? Are they Christians and, if so, how do you know?

   b. 1 Cor. 1:10-13—What was going on in the church at Corinth, and what did Paul encourage them to do?

   c. Have you ever been part of a church or Bible study like the one you just read about? If so, describe briefly the effect it had upon you and/or the church.

2. Find out more about the people of the church of Corinth by reading 1 Corinthians 3:1-4, then answer the following questions:

### 1 Corinthians 3:1-4

¹ Dear brothers and sisters, when I was with you I couldn't talk to you as I would to spiritual people. I had to talk as though you belonged to this world or as though you were infants in the Christian life.

² I had to feed you with milk, not with solid food, because you weren't ready for anything stronger. And you still aren't ready,

³ for you are still controlled by your sinful nature. You are jealous of one another and quarrel with each other. Doesn't that prove you are controlled by your sinful nature? Aren't you living like people of the world?

⁴ When one of you says, "I am a follower of Paul," and another says, "I follow Apollos," aren't you acting just like people of the world?

a. What previous problems had Paul experienced with the people of the church at Corinth when he was with them in person (vs. 1-2)?

b. Did the people change after Paul left them (vs. 2b-3)? Why or why not? What was their root problem?

c. What specific problems did the people have with one another?

d. How were the people of the church at Corinth living and acting (vs. 3b-4)?

3. Although you will not find the phrase "Casual Christian" in the Bible, you will find the word "carnal" in the King James Version of 1 Corinthians 3:1-4. See for yourself by reading the passage from the KJV and circling the word "carnal" each time it is used.

### 1 Corinthians 3:1-4 (KJV)

¹ *And I, brethren, could not speak unto you as unto spiritual, but as unto carnal, even as unto babes in Christ.*

² *I have fed you with milk, and not with meat: for hitherto ye were not able to bear it, neither yet now are ye able.*

³ *For ye are yet carnal: for whereas there is among you envying, and strife, and divisions, are ye not carnal, and walk as men?*

⁴ *For while one saith, I am of Paul; and another, I am of Apollos; are ye not carnal?*

"Carnal" isn't a very familiar word to most people, so in this study I will refer to carnal Christians as "Casual Christians," and I think it's appropriate. Because as you are about to see, carnal Christians are very casual in their commitment and obedience to Christ.

4. 1 Corinthians 3:1-4 describes some of the characteristics of carnality/casual Christianity. Create a descriptive list of them.

5. Read the following definitions of the word "carnal," then complete the sentence in "d":

a. This is a very simple definition of "carnal":

Persons under the influence of fleshly appetites; coveting and living for the things of this life.[7]

b. In this quotation by Albert Barnes, the word "natural" (used in 1 Cor. 2:14) is also defined:

The word *carnal* here is not the same which in 1 Corinthians 2:14 is translated *natural*. That refers to one who is unrenewed [unsaved; a non-Christian], and who is wholly under the influence of his sensual or animal nature, and is nowhere applied to Christians. This is applied here to Christians, but to those who have much of the remains of corruption, and who are imperfectly acquainted with the nature of religion; babes in Christ…[In 1 Cor. 3:1-4] it denotes that they were as yet under the influence of the corrupt passions and desires which the flesh produces.[8]

c. This quotation by Warren Wiersbe is very helpful in defining the "natural" person, the "spiritual" person, and the "carnal" person—all three of which Paul refers to in 1 Corinthians 1-3:

> Paul already explained that there are two kinds of people in the world—natural (unsaved) and spiritual (saved). But now [in 1 Cor. 3:1-4] he explained that there are two kinds of saved people: mature and immature (carnal). A Christian matures by allowing the Spirit to teach him and direct him by feeding on the Word. The immature Christian lives for the things of the flesh (carnal means "flesh") and has little interest in the things of the Spirit. Of course, some believers are immature because they have been saved only a short time, but that is not what Paul is discussing here.[9]

d. Considering all that you've just read, compose your own definition of *carnal* by completing the following sentence:

When Paul describes the people of the church at Corinth as "carnal," it means they are

_____

_____

_____.

6. To review what you just learned, take a quick open book test. Read the following statements, compare them with 1 Corinthians 3:1-4 and the definitions in Question 5. Then circle whether they are true or false.

a. There are two types of Christians: spiritual and carnal.

    True       False

b. There are two types of Christians: spiritually mature and spiritually immature.

    True       False

c. There are two types of Christians: 1) those who are controlled by the Holy Spirit; 2) those who are controlled by their own fleshly appetites.

    True       False

d. Carnal Christians can often be identified by their behaviors, desires, and priorities.

    True       False

e. A carnal Christian is more conversant in worldly topics than in spiritual and biblical ones.

    True       False

7. Read the following passages from 1 Corinthians, and record some of the specific ways the people at the church of Corinth displayed carnality/casual Christianity:

a. 1 Cor. 5:1-6

b. 1 Cor. 6:1-7

c. 1 Cor. 6:15-18

d. 1 Cor. 11:20-22

*reflect*

8. Take a few moments to pause and reflect upon everything you've studied today and how it applies to you. Then check the box that best describes your current spiritual condition and fill in the blank.

☐ I am more spiritually mature than I have ever been, and it shows in my inward and outward life and lifestyle. God is, however, calling me to maturity and obedience to Him in the following areas:

_____

☐ I am not as spiritually mature as I have been in the past, and it shows in my inward and outward life and lifestyle. God is calling me to maturity and obedience to Him in the following areas:

_____

☐ I am a new Christian, but I am growing in spiritual maturity through God's Word. God is calling me to maturity and obedience to Him in the following areas:

_____

☐ I am a Christian, but I am a carnal/casual Christian. God is calling me to maturity and obedience to Him in the following areas of my life:

_____

## *day 5:* FOLLOW ME...EVEN WHEN YOU FAIL

"Who are you kidding? You? A disciple? You're just another wannabe."

"Remember the last time you got all fired-up and committed to God? Two days later, and you were back to the same ol' you."

"Count the cost. Carry your cross. Lose your life to find it. Just think of all of the things you're going to have to give up. You know you don't want to."

"Quit now. The more you study, the worse you're going to feel about yourself."

"C'mon, you're already a pretty good Christian. And you're a much better one than your husband/boyfriend/girlfriend/co-worker/neighbor/etc."

"You're way too busy right now to keep doing that Bible study. You'll have a lot more time to do it when you _____ (fill in the blank with any number of excuses)."

Did the enemy take any potshots at you like that this week? Do you know what that means? It means, my dear sister, that you are making spiritual progress.

Surprised? I know. All of that condemnation, intimidation, temptation, and lie after lie after lie can really wear you down. It can even convince you that you're a complete failure when you are so not.

But just in case you're still skeptical of your own spiritual progress, I'm going to allow someone else to prove my point. Enjoy your study today of one of the most famous failures, devoted disciples, and spiritual success stories ever: Peter.

1. Read Matthew 16:13-20, and record what Peter did and what Jesus promised him.

2. Read Matthew 16:21-23, and record what Peter did and how Jesus responded.

3.  Read Matthew 26:31-35, and record both of Peter's responses to Jesus.

4.  Read Matthew 26:36-46, and record what Peter did only a few short hours before Jesus' arrest and crucifixion.

5.  As if it couldn't get any worse for Peter, read John 18:2-11 and Luke 22:51. Record what Peter did and how Jesus responded.

6.  Peter's lowest point and greatest failure is recorded in Matthew 26:69-75. Read the account and respond below:

    a.  Describe what Peter did and how this affected him.

    b.  Put yourself in Peter's sandals. What potshots do you think the enemy took against Peter?

7.  Your final passage of study today is John 21:15-22. This takes place after the resurrection. Read the passage and record how Jesus deals with Peter even after all of his past failures.

*reflect*

8. What did you learn from Peter's relationship to Jesus that you can apply to your own relationship with Christ?

_____

_____

_____

_____

_____

_____

*The wonder of it all is that Jesus called men like [the disciples]. I have always felt that since He called imperfect men like the disciples were, He may be able to use me, and He may be able to use you. It is encouraging to know that we don't have to be super-duper saints to be used by Him. He may not make you a fisher of men, if you are not in the fishing business. But whatever business you are engaged in, He can use you. Whatever your talent may be, if you will turn it over to Him, He can use it. Years ago a lady in my church was absolutely tongue-tied when it came to witnessing for Christ, but she could bake the most marvelous cakes! She used to deplore the fact of her inability to witness, and I said to her one day, 'Did it ever occur to you that the Lord may want you in the church family to bake cakes?' That may seem ridiculous, but it is not. The important thing for us is to give ourselves to Him. Under His direction He won't have us all doing the same thing because He gives us separate gifts. The body of Christ has many members in it, and they all have different functions to perform.*

—J. Vernon McGee, *Thru the Bible with J. Vernon McGee*[10]

are you a DISCIPLE?

# Devoted Disciples vs. Casual Christians

The _____ of _____: _Matt. 11:29-30_

1. _____-_____ _Luke 9:23-24_

2. _____ _Luke 9:23, 1:38_

3. _____ _____ _Luke 14:26_

4. _____ _Luke 14:33_

The _____ of Casual Christians:

1. _____/Spiritual _____ _1 Cor. 3:1-2_

2. _____ by their _____ _____ _1 Cor. 3:3-4, 2 Tim. 4:10-11_

### Philippians 3:10-12 (NKJV)

_That I may know Him and the power of His resurrection, and the fellowship of His sufferings, being conformed to His death, if, by any means, I may attain to the resurrection from the dead. Not that I have already attained, or am already perfected; but I press on, that I may lay hold of that for which Christ Jesus has also laid hold of me._

Discipleship requires _____.     True     False

Discipleship requires _____ _____.     True     False

# week 3

# DEVOTED DISCIPLE: DISTINCTIVES 1 & 2

*As a general guideline, we discovered that the typical disciple [in the churches we studied] devotes an average of four to six hours per week, beyond attending the worship service, to spiritual development efforts.*

— George Barna, *Growing True Disciples*[1]

# *day 1*: OVERVIEWING THE WEEKS AHEAD

I love the quote you just read by George Barna. But when I first saw it in his book, *Growing True Disciples*, I was a little unnerved—the "four to six hours per week" discovery sounded waaaay too low to me.

After all, the requirements Jesus set for discipleship are high. And as every good perfectionist knows, "high" means exerting enormous amounts of time and energy attempting to accomplish something in which you will still fall short. Alas, perfectionism never fails to disappoint.

But thank God for Barna's research on discipleship. In interviews with hundreds of Christians and non-Christians nationwide, pastors from over 600 Protestant churches, and information gleaned from pastors and churches who are well-known for their strong discipleship programs, Barna and his team have given us (especially us perfectionists) some marvelous news:[2]

The requirements for discipleship are high, but **becoming a disciple is attainable**.

Not only is it attainable, four to six hours per week devoted "to spiritual development efforts" is doable – especially if you're actively involved in a Bible study *like you are right now*. Precious sister, it makes me so happy to tell you that you are well on your way to becoming a true disciple of Jesus Christ (and I hope that you're smiling like I am right now).

Today you will overview the 7 Distinctives of Devoted Disciples. These seven distinctives, or unique characteristics, typify true disciples—and you'll be pleased to know that studying the Bible is one of them. For the next several weeks, you will be studying each of these distinct characteristics in detail.

But before you begin, would you mind if I repeated something I said earlier? Thanks. Here goes:

The requirements for discipleship are high, **but becoming a disciple is attainable**.

Like music to a perfectionist's ear.

1. Use your Bible to locate each passage on the following chart, and record it word-for-word in the space provided. Then in the right-hand column, summarize each distinctive in as few words as possible. To help you get started, Distinctive # 1 has been provided for you as an example.

## The 7 Distinctives of Devoted Disciples

| | |
|---|---|
| John 8:31 | Distinctive # 1<br>A disciple knows and obeys God's Word. |
| John 8:32 | Distinctive # 2 |
| Acts 1:4-5, 8 | Distinctive # 3 |
| Luke 18:1 | Distinctive # 4 |
| John 15:8 | Distinctive # 5 |
| John 13:34-35 | Distinctive # 6 |
| Luke 6:40 | Distinctive # 7 |

2.  Take a few minutes to prayerfully review your chart of the 7 Distinctives of Devoted Disciples. Evaluate your own spiritual life in each of the seven areas, then complete the following sentences:

    a.  The two strongest distinctives I am experiencing in my own life now seem to be

    _____ and _____ , and the reason

    I believe these areas are stronger is because _____

    _____.

    b.  The two weakest distinctives in my own spiritual life now seem to be _____

    and _____, and the reason I believe these areas are weaker is

    because _____.

In Day Two through Five of this week's homework, you will do an in-depth study of the first two distinctives. And as you may have already noticed, they are related. One depends upon the other. That's one of the beautiful things you will see about all seven of these distinctives. They all work together to make all of us like Jesus.

*reflect*

3.  Before you begin your in-depth study of The 7 Distinctives of Devoted Discipleship tomorrow, I want to share an encouraging verse with you (especially if you're prone to perfectionism):

    *For I am confident of this very thing, that He who began a*
    *good work in you will perfect it until the day of Christ Jesus.*

    — Philippians 1:6 (NASB)

Reflect upon that promise. Allow it to sink deep into your soul. Now express what Philippians 1:6 means to you by composing a brief prayer of praise to God.

_____

_____

## day 2: HUNGRY?

A hunger for God's Word was the very first tip-off that something radical had taken place in my life. I eagerly embraced it as a sweet gift and confirmation of God's gracious new beginning for me.

But the Bible is a big book. I didn't know where to dive in. So, propped up by several pillows in my bed that morning and hungry to be fed, I silently inquired, "Lord, where do I start? Genesis? It's been a long time since I've done this, and I'm overwhelmed."

"Matthew. Begin in Matthew." God was speaking to me again! It was one more confirmation that the brokenness I had experienced the day before was the beginning of something new and not just some hormonally induced, emotional meltdown.

Getting into The Gospels was just what I needed. It was like getting to know Jesus all over again. I only read one chapter each day, but it was so satisfying. God's Word filled me and strengthened me and gave me hope for a marriage that was hanging on by a thread.

Several years later, as I was having my quiet time, I came across a verse that perfectly described what God had done in my broken past:

> *He humbled you and let you be hungry, and fed you with manna which you did not know, nor did your fathers know, that He might make you understand that man does not live by bread alone, but man lives by everything that proceeds out of the mouth of the LORD.*
>
> —Deuteronomy 8:3 (NASB)

Precious sister, has God ever humbled you? Has He ever let you be hungry? The only reason He does that is because He wants you to discover that nothing can ever satisfy, strengthen, fill, and encourage you like His Word can. There are no substitutes. None.

So, dive in to God's Word today. Enjoy a good meal. Hope you're hungry.

1. Yesterday, you created an overview of The 7 Distinctives of Devoted Disciples, and you discovered Distinctive #1 in John 8:31. Review that verse again and compare it to several translations. Then answer the questions that follow.

   **John 8:31 (KJV)**
   *Then said Jesus to those Jews which believed on him, If ye continue in my word, then are ye my disciples indeed;*

   **John 8:31 (NLT)**
   *Jesus said to the people who believed in him, "You are truly my disciples if you remain faithful to my teachings."*

   **John 8:31 (AMP)**
   *So Jesus said to those Jews who had believed in Him, If you abide in My word [hold fast to My teachings and live in accordance with them], you are truly My disciples.*

   a. Who was Jesus addressing in this verse? Circle your answer.

   Believers/Christians          Unbelievers/non-Christians

b.  According to Jesus, are all believers disciples? Circle your answer.

Yes          No

c.  According to Jesus, a true disciple will know and obey His Word.

True          False

2.  Contrast what you just read and learned with a Casual Christian and their relationship with God's Word. Read the following passage (also included in last week's homework), and answer the questions that follow.

### 1 Corinthians 3:1-3

¹  *Dear brothers and sisters, when I was with you I couldn't talk to you as I would to spiritual people. I had to talk as though you belonged to this world or as though you were infants in the Christian life.*

²  *I had to feed you with milk, not with solid food, because you weren't ready for anything stronger. And you still aren't ready,*

³  *for you are still controlled by your sinful nature. You are jealous of one another and quarrel with each other. Doesn't that prove you are controlled by your sinful nature? Aren't you living like people of the world?*

a.  Who was Paul addressing in this verse? Circle your answer.

Believers/Christians          Unbelievers/Non-Christians

b.  According to what Jesus said in John 8:31, were the church members in Corinth disciples? Circle your answer.

Yes          No

c.  According to Paul, these church members in Corinth were not growing in their knowledge of God's Word nor were they obeying it. Circle your answer.

True          False

John 8:31 and 1 Corinthians 3:1-3 reveal Distinctive #1 of a Devoted Disciple and a Casual Christian:

| DEVOTED DISCIPLE | CASUAL CHRISTIAN |
| --- | --- |
| Distinctive # 1:<br>Knows and obeys God's Word.<br>—*John 8:31* | Distinctive # 1:<br>Doesn't know or obey God's Word.<br>—*1 Cor. 3:1-3* |

3. Using your Bible, read each of the following passages and record what you learn from Jesus about His Word:

   a. Matthew 4:1-4 (this will be familiar to you)

   b. Matthew 24:35

   c. Mark 8:38

   d. John 15:3, 17:17

4. Using your Bible, read each of the following passages. Record what you learn from Jesus about the relationship between the Word and obedience.

   a. Matthew 7:24-27

   b. Luke 11:27-28

5. Using your Bible, read each of the following passages. Record what you learn from Jesus about His relationship with those who obey and disobey His Word.

   a. Luke 8:19-21

b. John 8:43-47

c. John 14:15, 21, 23-24

*reflect*

6. You have done the work of a disciple today by abiding in His Word. What differences do you notice in your life and relationships when you spend consistent time in God's Word? Reflect upon that question and record your insights.

_____

_____

_____

_____

# *day* 3: DISTRACTED?

*Many of His disciples withdrew and were not walking with Him anymore.*
— John 6:66 NASB

It was a turning point in Jesus' ministry. Things appeared to be heading south, and the Casual Christians of that day were beginning to bail. At that moment, Jesus turned to The Twelve and asked a very vulnerable, heart-wrenching question: "You do not want to go away also do you?" (John 6:67 NASB)

Thank God for Peter. Without leaving Jesus hanging for even a single second of awkward silence, Peter responded with pure authenticity, "Lord, to whom shall we go? You have the words of eternal life" (John 6:68 NASB). Don't you just want to hug him?

We live in a culture of Casual Christianity—even in the church. In this high-tech age of non-stop news, infinite internet access, and hundreds of cable and satellite TV channels at our fingertips, there are endless distractions to deter us from devoted discipleship—even when we're trying to do Bible study.

So today, as you work on your Bible study, I want you to do two things each time you get distracted or you're tempted to bail:

1) **Remind yourself of Jesus' question:** "You do not want to go away also do you?" (John 6:67 NASB).

2) **Repeat Peter's answer:** "Lord, to whom shall we go? You have the words of eternal life" (John 6:68 NASB).

Just doing my part to keep you running with the right crowd. Enjoy your study!

1. Yesterday, you studied John 8:31 where Jesus said, "You are truly my disciples if you remain faithful to my teachings." Some translations use the phrase "abide in my Word" or "continue in my Word."

The Greek word for abide/continue/and remain is *meno*, and it means "remaining steadfast, persevering."[3] But the real question is how in the world do you really do that? Discover for yourself by reading each passage on the following chart and recording what you learn.

## My Responsibilities to Know God's Word

|  | |
|---|---|
| 2 Timothy 2:15 | |
| Titus 2:5 | |
| James 1:22-23 | |
| 1 Peter 2:2 | |
| 1 John 2:4-6 | |

2. What happens when a Christian fails in their responsibilities to know God's Word? Does Casual Christianity only affect the Casual Christian? Read Hebrews 5:12-14 (which is a very accurate description of a Casual Christian), and answer the questions that follow:

### Hebrews 5:12-14

12 *You have been believers so long now that you ought to be teaching others. Instead, you need someone to teach you again the basic things about God's word. You are like babies who need milk and cannot eat solid food.*

13 *For someone who lives on milk is still an infant and doesn't know how to do what is right.*

14 *Solid food is for those who are mature, who through training have the skill to recognize the difference between right and wrong*

a. What should every believer eventually be able to do?

b. What are the dangers of not progressing in the knowledge of God's Word?

c. How could these dangers trickle down and affect our families and other relationships?

d. How could these dangers trickle down and affect the church?

e. How could these dangers trickle down and affect our country and even the world?

3. You've seen results of Casual Christianity. Now study the results of a Devoted Disciple. Read each passage on the following chart, and record the results of abiding in God's Word:

## The Results of Knowing God's Word

| Acts 20:32 | |
|---|---|
| Romans 10:17 | |
| Ephesians 5:25-27 | |
| 2 Timothy 3:16-17 | |
| 1 Peter 2:2 | |
| 1 John 2:5 | |

4. One of the best illustrations of a Devoted Disciple is found in Luke 10:38-42. Read this passage and, as you read, visualize the scene that it paints. Do your best to be a "fly on the wall" inside the home of these two sisters. Then record your answers to the following questions:

a. How did Mary demonstrate Distinctive #1 of a Devoted Disciple?

b. What price was Mary willing to pay in order to do what she did? Remember what you learned about the cost and requirements for discipleship in Week Two.

c. What made Martha choose and behave like a Casual Christian that day?

d. Describe your most recent "Martha Moment" and the results of your choice.

e. Describe your most recent "Mary Moment" and the results of your choice.

*reflect*

5. Reflect upon Jesus' words to Martha in Luke 10:41-42, then do what Mary did. Literally. Sit on the floor (if you are physically able) in Jesus' presence for at least five minutes and listen. Give Him your undivided, undistracted attention. Record anything you learn at His feet.

_____

_____

_____

_____

_____

_____

# day 4: FREEDOM!

It's one of the most well-known and oft-quoted verses in the entire Bible: "And ye shall know the truth, and the truth shall make you free" (John 8:32 KJV).

But most people who quote John 8:32 have no idea that:

- They are quoting Jesus.
- The "truth" Jesus speaks of is "God's revelation to people."[4]
- The freedom Jesus promises is "true spiritual freedom from sin and death."[5]

The most vital point, however, that even most Christians don't know about John 8:32 is this:

- The promise does belong to Christians, but *only* to those who are disciples.

John 8:32 is not a one-size-fits-all verse. But for the disciple, it is a perfect fit.

1. Today, you will begin studying Distinctive #2 of the 7 Distinctives of Devoted Disciples. It's found in John 8:32, the verse you read in the introduction to this lesson. Please read it in context (with the verses that precede it) from each translation, and answer the questions that follow.

   **John 8:30-32 (KJV)**
   *30 As he spake these words, many believed on him.*
   *31 Then said Jesus to those Jews which believed on him, If ye continue in my word, then are ye my disciples indeed;*
   *32 And ye shall know the truth, and the truth shall make you free.*

   **John 8:30-32 (NLT)**
   *30 Then many who heard him say these things believed in him.*
   *31 Jesus said to the people who believed in him, "You are truly my disciples if you remain faithful to my teachings.*
   *32 And you will know the truth, and the truth will set you free."*

   a. According to verse 30, what had just happened to the people Jesus was addressing?

b. When you consider what had just happened to them, why did Jesus likely tell them what He did in verses 31-32?

c. In both translations (including the original Greek translation), verse 32 begins with the same word. What is it, and why is it important?

2. What kind of freedom does the truth bring in the life of a disciple? Read the following notes from several sources, then record your answer to "d."

a. *The Complete Word Study Dictionary New Testament* defines the word "free" in John 8:32 as follows:

To make free, liberate from the power of sin, the result of redemption.[6]

b. In *The Bible Exposition Commentary*, Warren Wiersbe says:

In the previous verses, Jesus addressed the "believers" mentioned in John 8:30, and He warned them that continuance in the Word—discipleship—was proof of true salvation. When we obey His Word, we grow in spiritual knowledge; and as we grow in spiritual knowledge, we grow in freedom from sin. Life leads to learning, and learning leads to liberty.[7]

c. In *The Teacher's Commentary*, Lawrence O. Richards says:

To be "free" is not to live selfishly, doing whatever one wants whenever one wants, but to live a disciplined and godly life which releases us from our bondage to sin so that the choices we make lead to what helps us rather than to what hurts. All this can be found if we are only willing to really be the disciples of Jesus.[8]

d. As you consider everything you've just read, what kind of freedom will a disciple of Jesus experience?

3. Contrast what you just read and learned with a Casual Christian. Read 1 Corinthians 3:1-3 (you should be very familiar with it now), and answer the questions that follow.

**1 Corinthians 3:1-3**

¹ *Dear brothers and sisters, when I was with you I couldn't talk to you as I would to spiritual people. I had to talk as though you belonged to this world or as though you were infants in the Christian life.*

² *I had to feed you with milk, not with solid food, because you weren't ready for anything stronger. And you still aren't ready,*

³ *for you are still controlled by your sinful nature. You are jealous of one another and quarrel with each other. Doesn't that prove you are controlled by your sinful nature? Aren't you living like people of the world?*

a. Will a Casual Christian experience freedom from sin? Circle your answer.

   Yes      No

b. What controls a Casual Christian?

c. What is the proof of that control?

John 8:32 and 1 Corinthians 3:1-3 reveal Distinctive #2 of a Devoted Disciple and a Casual Christian:

| DEVOTED DISCIPLE | CASUAL CHRISTIAN |
|---|---|
| Distinctive # 2: | Distinctive # 2: |
| Free from their sinful nature. | Bound to their sinful nature. |
| —*John 8:32* | —*1 Cor. 3:1-3* |

4. The phrase "sinful nature" is translated "carnal" in the King James Version. You studied what carnality means in Week 2, Day 4, Question 5. Review those notes now to refresh your understanding of what the "sinful nature" is.

5.  Many times in the New Testament, you will see the word "flesh," but it means the same thing as "carnal" and "sinful nature." Read the following passages, and record what Jesus taught about the flesh.

    a.  Matthew 26:38-41

    b.  John 3:1-7 ("flesh" is used in v. 6)

        **NOTE:**   In verse 5, "born of water and the Spirit" refers to physical birth and spiritual birth. Most theologians believe the water connotes a mother's water breaking before she gives birth.

Today's homework has been very technical. I hope I haven't worn you out. My goal is to encourage you to develop good observation and interpretation skills when you are reading and studying the Word which will ultimately lead to good application of the Word to your life. Bless you for pressing through! Conclude your study now with some very practical application.

*reflect*

6.  When you look back at your own walk and history with Jesus, what are some of the specific ways He has set you free? When you think about your walk with Him right now, in what specific areas of your life is He calling you to freedom from your flesh? Record your answers to both of these questions.

    _____

    _____

    _____

    _____

# day 5: PROGRESS NOT PERFECTION

Did you notice the title of today's lesson? Do you like it as much as I do? I think I may need to tattoo it to my right hand.

The truth is, perfectionism is a big ol' bully that will push you around, pressure you to perform, and punch you in the gut every single time you do.

Thank God the goal of discipleship is *not* perfectionism. It is progress, and that progress is the process of sanctification. It's what Paul described so passionately when he said, "And we all, with unveiled face, beholding the glory of the Lord, are being transformed into the same image from one degree of glory to another. For this comes from the Lord who is the Spirit" (1 Cor. 3:18 ESV).

The process of sanctification—the supernatural work of the Holy Spirit that transforms and matures us little by little into the likeness of Christ—will continue throughout our lifetime. But when that life is over, "**we shall be like Him** because we shall see Him just as He is" (1 John 3:2 NASB).

Perfection. It is our future. But for now, progress.

1.  Yesterday you learned Distinctive #2 of a Devoted Disciple and a Casual Christian. Do you remember what they were? If so, fill in the blanks in the box below. If not, review your Day Four homework, then fill in the blanks.

| DEVOTED DISCIPLE | CASUAL CHRISTIAN |
|---|---|
| Distinctive # 2: | Distinctive # 2: |
| _____ from their _____ _____. | _____ to their _____ _____. |
| —*John 8:32* | —*1 Cor. 3:1-3* |

2.  You already studied what Jesus said in John 8:32. Now take a look at what He said only four verses later by reading John 8:36 and recording it word-for-word below.

Freedom is a wonderful thing. But even here in America—the land of the free and the home of the brave—you and I are responsible for protecting the freedoms for which others fought and died. Otherwise, apathy will lead to slavery.

The same is true of our freedom in Christ. If we do not protect it by knowing and obeying His Word, we will become just like the Casual Christians in Corinth and live like slaves to our sinful nature.

3. You studied the importance of abiding in God's Word in your Day Two and Three homework. What else can you do to protect the freedom Christ died to give you? Read the following passages, and record what you learn about your responsibility as a disciple.

   a. Galatians 5:1

   b. Galatians 5:13

   c. Galatians 5:16

   d. Galatians 5:24-25 (Note how this passage parallels the requirements for discipleship.)

   e. Philippians 3:3

Remember what I told you yesterday about my goal to help you develop good observation and interpretation skills when you read and study your Bible? Prepare for a little more exercise, because the remainder of your homework will hone those skills and strengthen your spiritual muscles as a disciple.

4. One of the lifelong battles you will face as a disciple is the war between your sinful nature (the flesh) and the Spirit within you. Romans 8:1-16 is one of the premier passages about both and it is printed for you on the following page. Use the following instructions to help you observe, interpret, and understand what Romans 8 teaches about the sinful nature and the Holy Spirit.

   • Begin your observations by reading through the entire passage. As you read, circle the words "Spirit" and "Holy Spirit" each time you see them. Draw a box around the words "sin" and "sinful nature" each time you see them.

   • In the margin beside the passage, make two lists. Title the top list "The Spirit" and title second list (below it) "The Sinful Nature."

   • Read through the entire passage again and, using words from the text, record what you learn about the Spirit in the top list. Then record your findings about sin and the sinful nature in the bottom list. Number each entry and also include the verse number.

**Romans 8:1-16**

1 *So now there is no condemnation for those who belong to Christ Jesus.*

2 *And because you belong to him, the power of the life-giving Spirit has freed you from the power of sin that leads to death.*

3 *The law of Moses was unable to save us because of the weakness of our sinful nature. So God did what the law could not do. He sent his own Son in a body like the bodies we sinners have. And in that body God declared an end to sin's control over us by giving his Son as a sacrifice for our sins.*

4 *He did this so that the just requirement of the law would be fully satisfied for us, who no longer follow our sinful nature but instead follow the Spirit.*

5 *Those who are dominated by the sinful nature think about sinful things, but those who are controlled by the Holy Spirit think about things that please the Spirit.*

6 *So letting your sinful nature control your mind leads to death. But letting the Spirit control your mind leads to life and peace.*

7 *For the sinful nature is always hostile to God. It never did obey God's laws, and it never will.*

8 *That's why those who are still under the control of their sinful nature can never please God.*

9 *But you are not controlled by your sinful nature. You are controlled by the Spirit if you have the Spirit of God living in you. (And remember that those who do not have the Spirit of Christ living in them do not belong to him at all.)*

10 *And Christ lives within you, so even though your body will die because of sin, the Spirit gives you life because you have been made right with God.*

11 *The Spirit of God, who raised Jesus from the dead, lives in you. And just as God raised Christ Jesus from the dead, he will give life to your mortal bodies by this same Spirit living within you.*

12 *Therefore, dear brothers and sisters, you have no obligation to do what your sinful nature urges you to do.*

13 *For if you live by its dictates, you will die. But if through the power of the Spirit you put to death the deeds of your sinful nature, you will live.*

14 *For all who are led by the Spirit of God are children of God.*

15 *So you have not received a spirit that makes you fearful slaves. Instead, you received God's Spirit when he adopted you as his own children. Now we call him, "Abba, Father."*

16 *For his Spirit joins with our spirit to affirm that we are God's children.*

5. Complete the following sentence: *My favorite verse from Romans 8:1–16 is _____ because...*

*reflect*

6. Romans 13:14 says, "Put on the Lord Jesus Christ, and make no provision for the flesh, to gratify its desires" (ESV). In the war between the Holy Spirit and your sinful nature, what are the top two ways your sinful nature wants to control you? What practical steps can you take to "make no provision . . . to gratify its desires" and be free? Record your answers.

_____

_____

_____

_____

_____

_____

*One of the true marks of our ongoing sanctification is the growing awareness of how far short we fall of reaching perfection.*

— R. C. Sproul, *The Heresy of Perfectionism*[9]

are you a DISCIPLE?

# What does Jesus Believe About the Bible?

1. It is _____ _____. *Matt. 4:4*

2. It is a _____ _____ to wield against the enemy. *Matt. 4:1-11, Phil. 4:6-7*

3. It teaches us we are to worship _____ _____. *Matt. 4:10*

4. It will all be _____. *Matt. 5:18, 2 Peter 3:3-4*

5. The literal stories of: _____ and the flood; _____ and Gomorrah; and _____ and the fish. *Matt. 24:37-39, 10:15, 12:38-41*

6. God is _____; _____ between man and woman. *Matt. 19:4-5*

7. There is _____ after _____. *Matt. 22:31-32*

8. The Law and the _____ (the entire Old Testament). *Matt. 22:31-40*

9. _____ and all of the prophets spoke of Him. *Luke 24:25-27, 32*

10. In His _____ _____ after the tribulation. *Matt. 24:29-30*

**1 Peter 3:14-15 (NASB)**

*But even if you should suffer for the sake of righteousness, you are blessed. AND DO NOT FEAR THEIR INTIMIDATION, AND DO NOT BE TROUBLED, but sanctify Christ as Lord in your hearts, always being ready to make a defense to everyone who asks you to give an account for the hope that is in you, yet with gentleness and reverence.*

# week 4

# DEVOTED DISCIPLE: DISTINCTIVES 3 & 4

*The promise of a Helper presupposes that we need help. This promise of a Helper was Jesus' way of tipping us off to one of the most profound truths concerning the Christian life – it's impossible!*

— Charles Stanley, *The Wonderful Spirit-Filled Life*[1]

# *day 1:* THE EXTRAORDINARY POWER OF THE ORDINARY DISCIPLE

Untrained and uneducated. That was the assessment of the well-trained, well-educated crowd regarding the two former fishermen who stood on trial before them. Yet, as they listened to them speak, those same well-trained, well-educated religious leaders "were marveling and began to recognize them as having been with Jesus" (Acts 4:13 NASB).

How did two ordinary men—Peter and John—with no formal education or rabbinic training impress a tough crowd of Jewish priests, elders, and scribes? The answer is found in the description that precedes Peter's speech: "Then Peter, filled with the Holy Spirit, said to them…" (Acts 4:8 NASB).

The Holy Spirit empowers ordinary men and women to be used by God in extraordinary ways. Like the engine inside every car, the Holy Spirit is the power source within every believer.

Dear sister, perhaps you can relate to Peter and John. Maybe you lack formal training, education, a high school diploma, or a college degree. As you begin today's homework, remember this: whether you are trained or untrained, educated or not, the very same Holy Spirit who filled and empowered Peter and John fills and empowers you. Finally, be encouraged by the inspired words of the exceptionally well-trained and well-educated Apostle Paul:

> *Remember, dear brothers and sisters, that few of you were wise in the world's eyes or powerful or wealthy when God called you. Instead, God chose things the world considers foolish in order to shame those who think they are wise. And he chose things that are powerless to shame those who are powerful. God chose things despised by the world, things counted as nothing at all, and used them to bring to nothing what the world considers important. As a result, no one can ever boast in the presence of God.*
>
> —1 Corinthians 1:26-29

1.  Last week, you studied the first two Distinctives of Devoted Disciples and Casual Christians:

| DEVOTED DISCIPLE | CASUAL CHRISTIAN |
|---|---|
| Distinctive # 1:<br>Knows and obeys God's Word.<br>*—John 8:31* | Distinctive # 1:<br>Doesn't know or obey God's Word.<br>*—1 Cor. 3:1-3* |
| Distinctive # 2:<br>Free from their sinful nature.<br>*—John 8:32* | Distinctive # 2:<br>Bound to their sinful nature.<br>*—1 Cor. 3:1-3* |

This week you will study two more:

| DEVOTED DISCIPLE | CASUAL CHRISTIAN |
|---|---|
| Distinctive # 3:<br>Controlled and empowered<br>by the Holy Spirit.<br>*—Acts 1:8* | Distinctive # 3:<br>Controlled by their sinful nature.<br>*—1 Cor. 3:3-4* |
| Distinctive # 4:<br>Prays at all times.<br>*—Luke 18:1* | Distinctive # 4:<br>Prays now and then. |

2.  In the hours prior to His arrest and crucifixion, Jesus encouraged and prepared His disciples. Much of this preparation involved teaching them about the Holy Spirit. Using your Bible, read the following scriptures and record your answers to each question:

    **NOTE:** The King James Version of John 14:16, 26, 15:26, and 16:7 uses the word "Comforter" to describe the Holy Spirit/Holy Ghost. Other Bible translations of these same verses may use the word "Helper."

    a.  John 14:16-17 – How long will the Holy Spirit stay with you and where will He stay?

b.  John 14:26 – What will the Holy Spirit do?

c.  John 15:26 – Where does the Holy Spirit come from, and what will He do?

d.  John 16:7-8 – How does the Holy Spirit work in the world?

e.  John 16:13-14 – What will He do and not do?

3.  How have you experienced the work of the Holy Spirit in your life recently? How has He helped, taught, or spoken to you?

4.  You've seen what Jesus taught the disciples about the Holy Spirit prior to His arrest and crucifixion. Now study what He taught them after the resurrection. Using your Bible, read Acts 1:1-8, then record your answers to each question:

a.  What did Jesus command the disciples to do and why (v. 4)?

b.  What was about to happen to them and when (v. 5)?

c.  When the disciples received the Holy Spirit, what else would they receive and do (v. 8)?

5.  Are you experiencing the power of the Holy Spirit in your life? Check the box next to the description that best fits you.

☐  I consistently experience and depend upon the power of the Holy Spirit.

☐  I occasionally experience and depend upon the power of the Holy Spirit.

☐  I rarely experience and depend upon the power of the Holy Spirit.

6.  After Jesus' ascension (Acts 1:9), the promise of the Holy Spirit was fulfilled. Read Acts 2:1-4, and answer the question that follows.

**Acts 2:1-4**

¹  *On the day of Pentecost all the believers were meeting together in one place.*
²  *Suddenly, there was a sound from heaven like the roaring of a mighty windstorm, and it filled the house where they were sitting.*
³  *Then, what looked like flames or tongues of fire appeared and settled on each of them.*
⁴  *And everyone present was filled with the Holy Spirit and began speaking in other languages, as the Holy Spirit gave them this ability.*

Who received the Holy Spirit on the day of Pentecost? Circle your answer.

a)  the apostles        b)  some of the believers        c)  all of the believers

*reflect*

7. What two specific ways do you need the Holy Spirit's help and empowerment today? Record your answers, then submit yourself and your specific needs before the Lord in prayer. Allow the Holy Spirit to help and empower you today.

1) _____

2) _____

## *day* 2: POWER SHORTAGE?

It happened so slowly that I didn't even notice it at first. What I did notice, however, was how strained my eyes had become. "Maybe I need a new prescription for my glasses," I thought, "Or, maybe I just need to stop spending so much time on my computer." Meanwhile, I just kept plugging along writing this study in my cozy, messy home office.

Then one morning, Bill came into the kitchen where I was having breakfast and said, "Laurie, have you not noticed how dark your office is? I just went in there to use the printer, and two bulbs in that light fixture are out."

One step stool, two new bulbs, and a few minutes later, *voila!* The difference was dramatic. My eye strain soon disappeared, and (hallelujah) I didn't have to fork out major money for a new pair of glasses.

That same scenario can happen to us as disciples. We don't notice it at first, but one day or at some point, we stop depending upon the Holy Spirit to enlighten and empower us. We notice the symptoms—the stress and strain we are experiencing in our lives and relationships. But we just keep plugging on in our own strength, doing life, doing work, and doing our best.

**Warning**: It won't be long until others notice.

Today you will discover the symptoms of a spiritual power shortage in your life and how to experience on-going power. May you experience a Holy Spirit *voila* of power and light in your heart and life today!

1.  Yesterday you studied Jesus' promise of the Holy Spirit and the fulfilment of that promise (Acts 2:1-4) to the believers who were gathered together in Jerusalem on the day of Pentecost. You and I, of course, weren't part of that gathering. So, when and how did we receive the Holy Spirit? Discover the answer by reading Titus 3:5-6 and recording what you learn.

    **Titus 3:5-6**

    ⁵  he [God] saved us, not because of the righteous things we had done, but because of his mercy. He washed away our sins, giving us a new birth and new life through the Holy Spirit.
    ⁶  He generously poured out the Spirit upon us through Jesus Christ our Savior.

    When and how did you receive the Holy Spirit?

    Every Christian receives the Holy Spirit at salvation, but every Christian does not always experience the power of the Holy Spirit in their lives. Case in point: the Casual Christians described in 1 Corinthians.

    As I'm sure you will recall, the lives of the Casual Christians in Corinth were marked by quarreling, divisions, jealousy, strife, and even immorality (1 Corinthians 5), all of which are symptoms of a spiritual power shortage.

2.  Read the passage below and discover how a spiritual power shortage occurs. Note its negative symptoms and other results. Then answer the questions that follow.

    **Galatians 5:16-21**

    ¹⁶  So I say, let the Holy Spirit guide your lives. Then you won't be doing what your sinful nature craves.
    ¹⁷  The sinful nature wants to do evil, which is just the opposite of what the Spirit wants. And the Spirit gives us desires that are the opposite of what the sinful nature desires. These two forces are constantly fighting each other, so you are not free to carry out your good intentions
    ¹⁸  But when you are directed by the Spirit, you are not under obligation to the law of Moses
    ¹⁹  When you follow the desires of your sinful nature, the results are very clear: sexual immorality, impurity, lustful pleasures,
    ²⁰  idolatry, sorcery, hostility, quarreling, jealousy, outbursts of anger, selfish ambition, dissension, division,
    ²¹  envy, drunkenness, wild parties, and other sins like these. Let me tell you again, as I have before, that anyone living that sort of life will not inherit the Kingdom of God.

    a.   How does a spiritual power shortage occur (v. 17)?

    b.   What are the symptoms of a spiritual power shortage (vs. 19-21)? Underline each symptom within the text.

    c.   Have you experienced any of these symptoms in your life recently? Circle your answer.

           Yes, unfortunately, I have.        No, praise God, not lately.

    d.   Do you have enough personal strength and willpower to withstand and win the battle against your sinful nature? Circle your answer.

           Yes        No way, no how.

    e.   How have your own strength, willpower, and good intentions failed you recently? How have you experienced a power shortage?

    f.   How can you win the ongoing daily battle against your sinful nature (v. 16)?

3.   In next week's lesson, you will study the fruit of the Spirit (which is another Distinctive of Discipleship). Because the fruit of the Spirit also reveals the positive symptoms of the Spirit-filled and empowered life, take a brief look at them now. Read the following passage from Galatians 5:22-23, then answer the questions that follow.

### Galatians 5:22-23

[22] *But the Holy Spirit produces this kind of fruit in our lives: love, joy, peace, patience, kindness, goodness, faithfulness,*
[23] *gentleness, and self-control. There is no law against these things!*

a.  What are the symptoms of the Spirit-empowered life? Underline and number each of them within the text of Galatians 5:22-23.

b.  How are you experiencing the power and fruit of the Holy Spirit in your life? Of the nine fruits that are listed, identify the top three or four in which you experience the greatest degree of consistent power.

c.  Of the nine fruits that are listed, identify the top three or four in which you experience the most frequent power shortage.

4.  Galatians 5:22-23 is a must-memorize passage that will remind and encourage you to live the Spirit-filled life. It also will enable you to diagnose any possible power shortages in your life—and hopefully before others even notice.

So, right now, find two or three Post-it notes or note cards. Record Galatians 5:22-23 on each one of them. Then post them where you will see them throughout the day (on your mirror, refrigerator, the dashboard of your car, etc.). Your goal: to memorize the passage AND to allow the Holy Spirit to fill and empower you in such a way that you will produce each and every fruit.

*reflect*

5.  Spend a few moments in prayer before the Lord. Reflect upon what He has taught you today. Praise and thank Him for speaking to you, and if He has revealed any possible power shortages in your life—which, of course, is sin—confess and repent right now. Be sure also to confess and seek forgiveness from those who may have witnessed or been hurt by your sin. Finally, ask God to fill and empower you afresh and anew with the Holy Spirit, your divine Helper.

# *day 3:* UNMISTAKABLE, UNLIMITED POWER

*"You shall receive power when the Holy Spirit has come upon you; and you shall be My witnesses."*

—Acts 1:8 (NASB)

Sometimes we forget that one of the primary purposes of the power of the Holy Spirit is to make us witnesses of the One we follow. While it is true that others will notice when we fail to exercise that power—i.e., sin—they also will notice when we do exercise and are empowered by the Spirit.

Not long after Pentecost, Peter and John were heading to the temple to pray. But just as they were about to go inside, Peter healed a crippled beggar. Those who witnessed this miracle were surprised, and they quickly surrounded Peter, John and the man who had been healed.

Then Peter addressed the crowd and asked, "Why do you gaze at us, as if by our own power or piety we had made [this man] walk?" (Acts 3:12 NASB). That question was the beginning of Peter's second gospel sermon, and it resulted in the conversion of over 5000 men. But what had led them to even listen to that sermon was the unmistakable, unlimited power they witnessed upon Peter and John—the power of the Holy Spirit.

Today you will conclude your study of Distinctive #3 of Devoted Disciples: They are controlled and empowered by the Holy Spirit. Yes, a Devoted Disciple will experience power over their sinful nature, and yes, a Devoted Disciple will experience power to produce spiritual fruit. But never forget, that power is also an unmistakable witness to others of the unlimited power of the one and only God who saves.

1.  As you just read in Acts 1:8, Jesus said that the power of the Holy Spirit will enable you to be His witnesses. Using your own Bible, read the following verses. Record what God's power and the Holy Spirit will enable you to do and how you can apply it to your life and current circumstances.

    a.  Romans 15:13

    b   2 Timothy 1:7-8

c. 2 Peter 1:2-3

2. Ephesians 5:18-21 describes some of the most beautiful ways the infilling power of the Holy Spirit can be demonstrated in our lives. Read that passage and record what you learn about how to allow the Holy Spirit to flow through your life.

3. Just as we can allow the power of the Holy Spirit to flow freely in our lives, we also can do the opposite. Read the following passages, and record your answers to each question.

### Ephesians 4:29-32

29 *Don't use foul or abusive language. Let everything you say be good and helpful, so that your words will be an encouragement to those who hear them.*
30 *And do not bring sorrow to God's Holy Spirit by the way you live. Remember, he has identified you as his own, guaranteeing that you will be saved on the day of redemption.*
31 *Get rid of all bitterness, rage, anger, harsh words, and slander, as well as all types of evil behavior.*
32 *Instead, be kind to each other, tenderhearted, forgiving one another, just as God through Christ has forgiven you.*

### 1 Thessalonians 5:16-22

16 *Always be joyful.*
17 *Never stop praying.*
18 *Be thankful in all circumstances, for this is God's will for you who belong to Christ Jesus.*
19 *Do not stifle the Holy Spirit.*
20 *Do not scoff at prophecies,*
21 *but test everything that is said. Hold on to what is good.*
22 *Stay away from every kind of evil.*

a. There are two commands regarding the Holy Spirit in these passages. What are they?

b  As you look at the context of the command in Ephesians 4, what are some of the specific things that could cause you to break that command?

c. As you look at the context of the command in 1 Thessalonians 5, what are some of the specific things that could cause you to break that command?

*reflect*

4. There is one final reference regarding the Holy Spirit that I want you consider. It is Romans 14:17. Read and reflect upon it, then spend a few moments in prayer thanking God for all that He has given you through the indwelling power of the Holy Spirit.

*For the Kingdom of God is not a matter of what we eat or drink, but of living a life of goodness and peace and joy in the Holy Spirit.*

— Romans 14:17

## *day* 4: PRAYER 101

Her name is Dolly, and she is a prayer warrior. I know this not because she advertises her prayer prowess. I know because I have personally witnessed her consistency in prayer for well over 20 years.

Confirmation of Dolly's prayer warrior status arrives every day when I open my inbox and find an email from her like this:

**From:** Dolly
**Sent:** Thursday, August 28, 2014
**To:** Prayer Partner
**Subject:** Worship the LORD

Many of the verses in our prayers have to do with worshiping the LORD, especially on the Sabbath. You've probably figured out that I love to praise and worship our LORD! But, like most of you, waiting doesn't come naturally, we look for the shortest line, get behind the fastest vehicle, take the quickest route.

One of my favorite song lyrics is "I will worship while I'm waiting on You LORD". Let us worship Him while we wait.

Father, we worship and bow down, we kneel before You, LORD our Maker, [in reverent praise and supplication]. We worship toward Your holy temple and praise Your name for Your loving-kindness and for Your truth and faithfulness; for You have exalted Your name above all else and You have magnified Your Word above Your name! In the morning You hear our voices, O LORD, as we lay our requests before You and watch and wait [for You to speak to our hearts]. When we are in trouble we call on You because Your Word assures us that You will answer. We exalt You, LORD our God, and worship at Your feet, for You are holy! [Psalm 95:6, 138:2, 5:3, 86:7; 99:5 AMP]

Dolly prays God's Word, a powerful practice that honors the Lord and edifies those of us who are privileged to be her prayer partners. So, can you see now why I enjoy opening her emails so much?

When it comes to prayer, I will never be Dolly. But as a disciple, prayer is an essential part of my daily relationship with Jesus.

Today and tomorrow you will study some of the very same basics of prayer that Jesus taught to His disciples. Your homework will be light because I want you to practice what you learn by praying. In fact, why don't you begin right now by making this your prayer:

*"Lord, teach us to pray."* —Luke 11:1

1. Luke 18:1-8 is often called "The Parable of the Unjust Judge." In that parable, Jesus gives us some very practical instructions regarding prayer. Use your Bible to read it, then answer the following questions:

   a. What was Jesus' primary purpose in teaching this parable (v. 1)?

   b. Although God is certainly nothing like the unjust judge, what will He do when we consistently bring our needs before Him in prayer (vs. 7-8)?

   c. The most pressing need of the widow in this parable was legal protection. What about you? What is The Most Pressing Need in your life?

   d. How often are you bringing your most pressing need before the Lord in prayer? Circle your answer from the following list:

      • Every time I think about it.

      • Often, but probably not daily.

      • Occasionally, but not consistently.

2. In Matthew 6:5-8, Jesus taught a few of the basic dos and don'ts of prayer. Read this passage, and underline each instruction.

### Matthew 6:5-8

5 *"When you pray, don't be like the hypocrites who love to pray publicly on street corners and in the synagogues where everyone can see them. I tell you the truth, that is all the reward they will ever get.*

6 *But when you pray, go away by yourself, shut the door behind you, and pray to your Father in private. Then your Father, who sees everything, will reward you.*

7 *When you pray, don't babble on and on as people of other religions do. They think their prayers are answered merely by repeating their words again and again.*

8 *Don't be like them, for your Father knows exactly what you need even before you ask him!"*

3. In Question 1c, you identified your greatest prayer need. Now I want you to identify, perhaps, your greatest prayer challenge. Read Matthew 5:43-44, then record your answers to the questions that follow.

**Matthew 5:43-44**

⁴³ *"You have heard the law that says, 'Love your neighbor' and hate your enemy.*
⁴⁴ *But I say, love your enemies! Pray for those who persecute you!"*

a. What specific instruction regarding prayer did Jesus give in verse 44?

b. Who are your enemies—an ex-husband, a former friend, or maybe a relative? Who has hurt or persecuted you—your boss, a co-worker, a neighbor, or perhaps someone else? Record each of their first names or initials.

*reflect*

4. Now it's time to get down to business. Find a quiet, private place where you can meet with God (a walk-in closet is perfect), and spend some time with Him in prayer. If you need a little help, use the following instructions. If not, please do your best to apply all of the instructions you learned today regarding prayer.

- Begin with praise to God, followed by confession and repentance of any sin He may reveal to you.

- Continue in prayer by using all the tools and instructions you've studied today.

- Follow the example of the widow in Luke 18. Present your Most Pressing Need to the Lord in prayer.

- Transition your time of prayer as you intercede for your family and loved ones.

- Now intercede for "those who persecute you"—your enemies.

- Finally, ask the Lord to speak to you. Do not rush. Listen for His still, small voice.

- Conclude your prayer time by asking Him to fill and empower you with His Spirit and by thanking Him for hearing your prayer.

# *day* 5: AND GOD...

"Pray without ceasing" (1 Thess. 5:17). When I was young, I could not get my arms around that verse. It seemed impossible, and I remember thinking, "You cannot pray without ceasing."

Turns out, yes, you absolutely can. How? By learning the "And God Prayer." Allow me to illustrate.

As you're folding the laundry or paying bills, you remember your son who is away at college, so you simply and silently pray, "And God, right now please protect and encourage my son and remind Him that You are right there beside Him today."

A few minutes later, while you're listening to the evening news, you pick up where you left off in prayer again and say, "And God, I know You see each and every one of the Middle Eastern Christians and how they are being persecuted for their faith. Protect and provide for their every need, and allow them to experience Your supernatural peace and presence even in the midst of their suffering."

That same night as you're brushing your teeth, preparing to go to bed, and thinking about all of the responsibilities that will greet you in the morning, you quietly connect with Him again. "And God remind me first thing in the morning that You are the vine and I am the branch. Help me to abide in You and not respond to stress by trying to do life in my own strength."

And that, my dear sister, is the "And God Prayer."

Caution: The "And God Prayer" should not replace your usual prayer and quiet time. Think of it as a wonderful, practical tool that will allow you to extend your prayer time all throughout the day.

Pray without ceasing? Yes, you can!

1. The Lord's Prayer (Matthew 6:9-13) is the most well-known prayer in the Bible. It is also the tool Jesus used to teach His disciples how to pray.

   The first few words of the Lord's Prayer are printed for you below. Do your best to record the rest of it (or as much as you can) without looking at the next section of your homework (okay, if you need a little help, you can peek). Here goes:

   Our Father who art in heaven, _____

   _____

   _____

   _____

   _____

The Lord's Prayer is a model we can use to pray. You see, each section represents a basic component of prayer. When you add them all together, you have all of the scriptural essentials to pray just like Jesus taught His disciples.

So, what are the basic components of the Lord's Prayer? This is how I break it down, but you can certainly modify it in a way that makes better sense to you and helps you remember it:

- Adoration: *Our Father who art in heaven, Hallowed be Thy name.*

- Submission to His sovereignty: *Thy kingdom come. Thy will be done, On earth as it is in heaven.*

- Supplication and Intercession: *Give us this day our daily bread.*

- Confession and Forgiveness: *And forgive us our debts, as we also have forgiven our debtors.*

- Protection: *And do not lead us into temptation, but deliver us from evil.*

- Worship: *For Thine is the kingdom, and the power, and the glory forever. Amen.* (Matt. 6:9-13 NASB)

2. As you saw yesterday, Jesus taught His disciples to "pray at all times" (Luke 18:1 NASB). If you want to become His disciple, you must develop a strong, scriptural, and consistent prayer life.

   Your final assignment this week is to create and record a sincere, heartfelt prayer to God using all of the basic components from the Lord's Prayer. Begin now by picking up your pencil, allowing the Holy Spirit to help you, and writing out your prayer to God:

   _____

   _____

   _____

   _____

   _____

   _____

   _____

*reflect*

3. You've written the prayer. Now lift it up to the Lord by reading it to Him.

*Prayer is the secret weapon of the kingdom of God. It is like a missile that can be fired toward any spot on earth, travel undetected at the speed of thought, and hit its target every time. It can even be armed with a delayed detonation device. In His prayer of John 17, Jesus said, 'I do not pray for these alone, but also for those who will believe in Me through their word (John 17:20). ... The implications are staggering. We, too, can pray about things yet to happen, things, for instance, in the lives of our children—and their children. ...[But] there's more. Satan has no defense against this weapon; he does not have an anti-prayer missile.*

—Ron Dunn, *Don't Just Stand There Pray Something*[2]

are you a DISCIPLE?

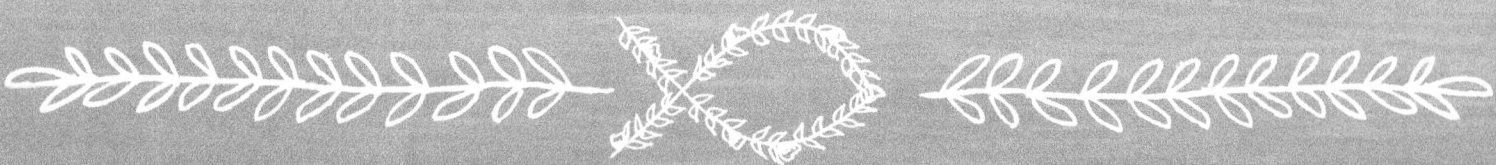

# Empowered!

*"But you will receive **power** when the Holy Spirit has come upon you;*
*and you shall be my witnesses both in Jerusalem, and in all Judea*
*and Samaria, and even to the remotest part of the earth."*
**Acts 1:8 (NASB)**

## The Holy Spirit Will Give You Power To:

1. _____ my _____. *Acts 1:8*

2. _____ in _____. *Rom. 15:13*

3. Do _____, _____ beyond all that you could ever ask or think.
   *Eph. 3:20*

4. Overcome _____ and _____. *2 Tim. 1:7*

5. _____ pertaining to life and godliness. *2 Pet. 1:3*

6. _____ and not _____ heart. *Luke 18:1*

## How to Experience This Power

1. Let the Holy Spirit _____ and _____ your life. *Gal. 5:16*

2. _____ the Spirit's _____. *Gal. 5:25*

3. _____ _____ with the Spirit. *Eph. 5:18*

4. Do not _____/_____ the Holy Spirit. *1 Thess. 5:19*

# DEVOTED DISCIPLE: DISTINCTIVES 5 & 6

*Abiding begins with visible spiritual disciplines, such as Bible reading and prayer. Yet it may shock you to find out that we can do these things for years without abiding. After all, reading a book about a person isn't the same thing as knowing the person who wrote the book. The challenge in abiding is always to break through from dutiful activities to a living, flourishing relationship with God.*

—Bruce Wilkinson, *Secrets of the Vine*[1]

# *day* 1: FRUIT IS YOUR FUTURE

We didn't have grass, and we didn't have landscaping. But what we did have when we moved to a small town just outside of Houston a few years ago was four acres of rough land and plenty of room to dream. And Bill had always dreamed of fruit trees.

So one Saturday morning, we piled into Bill's pick-up to pursue the dream. Later that evening, we returned home with our reward: a truck-load of peach, plum, lemon, and orange trees.

A few days later, those pretty little fruit trees dotted the back part of our property in raised beds Bill had lovingly prepared for them. When they bloomed a few weeks later and tiny fruit began to form and flourish, we rejoiced. Fruit was our future!

That happy ending, however, would be delayed.

You see, while researching online to find out how long it would take for our baby fruit to mature, we discovered some bad news. Turns out, first-year fruit should be pruned as soon as it appears because the only work a first-year fruit tree should do is develop its root system.

So, Bill did what he had to do. But his dream did not die. It was only delayed.

The following year, Bill's beloved trees produced a bumper crop (well, the citrus trees did; the pesky raccoons made off with our peach and plum crop). To this day I still have containers in my freezer filled with lemon and orange juice from that very first crop.

Perhaps you're wondering what my fruit tree story has to do with being a disciple. I could tell you, but Jesus can explain it even better. Join Him now in His Word as He shares the dream He has for your life—and fruit is a big part of it.

John 13-18:24 is a record of Jesus' final night with His disciples. It begins in the Upper Room as He shares a final meal with them. Then Jesus and the disciples leave the Upper Room and walk to the Garden of Gethsemane.

Along their way to the garden, however, they would very likely have seen vines growing on the city walls as well as vineyards nearby. Some theologians believe Jesus used these to illustrate something He taught His disciples that night *and* something He wants to teach you today as you study John 15:1-8.

1.      Read John 15:1-8, and complete the assignment and questions that follow.

### John 15:1-8 (NASB)

1   *"I am the true vine, and My Father is the vinedresser.*

2   *"Every branch in Me that does not bear fruit, He takes away; and every* branch *that bears fruit, He prunes it so that it may bear more fruit.*

3   *"You are already clean because of the word which I have spoken to you.*

4   *"Abide in Me, and I in you. As the branch cannot bear fruit of itself unless it abides in the vine, so neither* can *you unless you abide in Me.*

5   *"I am the vine, you are the branches; he who abides in Me and I in him, he bears much fruit, for apart from Me you can do nothing.*

6   *"If anyone does not abide in Me, he is thrown away as a branch and dries up; and they gather them, and cast them into the fire and they are burned.*

7   *"If you abide in Me, and My words abide in you, ask whatever you wish, and it will be done for you.*

8   *"My Father is glorified by this, that you bear much fruit, and so prove to be My disciples."*

a.  Draw a line matching the correct subject with the correct description:

| | |
|---|---|
| Jesus | branch |
| The disciple | vinedresser (one who cares for a vineyard)[2] |
| The Father | vine |

b.  What happens to a branch that does bear fruit and why?

c.  What is the only command in this parable?

d.  How can we know if we are obeying that command?

e.  How does the branch bear fruit, and what does that mean to us as Christians?

The word "abide" is, of course, a key repeated word in John 15. It also is used in John 8:31, and in your Week Three homework you learned that it means "remaining steadfast, persevering."[3]

But in the context of John 15, the word "abide" means "to remain in or with someone, i.e., to be and remain united with him, one in heart, mind, and will."[4] It also means "to keep in fellowship with Christ so that His life can work in and through us to produce fruit."[5]

2.  Sum up what it means to "abide in Christ" by circling the best definition from the following list:

    *   To abide is to work hard and do your best.
    *   To abide is to hang on for dear life.
    *   To abide is to pretty much do nothing.
    *   To abide is to remain in Christ and allow Him to do what we cannot do in and of ourselves: produce spiritual fruit.

3.  What is the promise and condition in John 15:7, and why do you think meeting that condition is essential to receiving the promise?

4.  What does bearing fruit prove?

Today you have discovered Distinctive #5 of Devoted Disciples:

> ### DEVOTED DISCIPLE
>
> Distinctive # 5:
> Bears much fruit.
> —*John 15:8*

5. Tomorrow you will continue your study on spiritual fruit. But for now, answer one final question: What does my story about Bill's fruit trees have in common with John 15:1-8?

*reflect*

6. Today's reflection will be a little different—and hopefully, a little fun, too.

   Take a small knife or an old pair of scissors, and go outside. Search your yard, garden, or outdoor area for several plant examples that are similar to the vine in John 15. Take a cutting from one or more of the examples you find (a flower from a bush, a limb from a shrub, etc.) and bring it inside.

   Place it where you will see it often (by your kitchen sink, on the table beside your favorite chair, etc.), but do not place it in a vase with water. Keep it this entire week, and observe how it slowly dries and eventually dies. Let it be a consistent reminder to you that "apart from Him, you can do nothing."

# *day 2:* NOURISHING & FLOURISHING

One of the biggest reasons Bill and I purchased the land where we now live is because the frontage of the property is home to over a dozen old, but still productive, native pecan trees. We love those trees and the shade and occasional fruit they produce. But we don't love the ongoing task of picking up the branches they shed on a constant basis—especially after a tough, Texas storm rolls through.

After a storm, the ground under our pecan trees is littered with branches. Some of them are often healthy and green. But we don't leave those branches lying there on the ground with the expectation that they will eventually sprout new leaves or produce new fruit. Branches apart from the tree can never produce a thing.

Branches, very simply, are the instruments the tree uses for bearing and producing fruit. The tree (or vine as in John 15) is the source that provides all the sap and nutrients necessary for the branch to bear fruit. The tree *produces* fruit. The branch only *bears* it.

Precious sister, Jesus does not command you to produce spiritual fruit. He does not even command you to bear fruit. Jesus does, however, command you to abide.

So today, do what a branch does best: abide. Be nourished through His Word, so that you will flourish with His fruit.

1.  Yesterday, as you studied John 15:1-8, you learned Distinctive #5 of Devoted Disciples: They bear much fruit. Part of that fruit, I believe, is the fruit of the Spirit which you studied last week from Galatians 5:22-23. Review that passage below, and circle each fruit of the Spirit.

### Galatians 5:22-23

²² *But the Holy Spirit produces this kind of fruit in our lives: love, joy, peace, patience, kindness, goodness, faithfulness,*
²³ *gentleness, and self-control. There is no law against these things!*

2.  Devoted Disciples bear spiritual fruit, but what about Casual Christians? Do they produce the fruit of the Spirit? To answer this question, think about what you have already learned about Casual Christianity from 1 Corinthians 1:10-13, 3:1-3 and what, perhaps, you have learned from your own experience as a Casual Christian. Then circle your answer.

No, never.          Maybe occasionally.          Yes, most of the time.

3. Just as the Holy Spirit produces spiritual fruit (Gal. 5:22-23), He also produces spiritual gifts (1 Cor. 12:4-11) such as prophecy, teaching, administration, helps, etc. Can Casual Christians produce spiritual gifts? Read and observe the following passage describing the Casual Christians at Corinth, then circle your answer to this question:

### 1 Corinthians 1:4-7

⁴ *I always thank my God for you and for the gracious gifts he has given you, now that you belong to Christ Jesus.*

⁵ *Through him, God has enriched your church in every way—with all of your eloquent words and all of your knowledge.*

⁶ *This confirms that what I told you about Christ is true.*

⁷ *Now you have every spiritual gift you need as you eagerly wait for the return of our Lord Jesus Christ.*

Yes, Casual Christians can produce spiritual gifts.

No, Casual Christians cannot produce spiritual gifts.

According to 1 Corinthians 1:4-7, the Holy Spirit was obviously enabling the Casual Christians at the church in Corinth to exercise their spiritual gifts. But 1 Cor. 1:10-13 and 3:1-3 reveals their spiritual fruit was in short supply. Therefore, Distinctive #5 of the Casual Christian is very different from the Devoted Disciple:

| DEVOTED DISCIPLE | CASUAL CHRISTIAN |
|---|---|
| Distinctive # 5:<br>Bears much fruit.<br>—John 15:8 | Distinctive # 5:<br>Bears little fruit.<br>—1 Cor. 1:10-13 |

4. What about you and your own Christian service and gifts? Have you ever served the Lord with your gifts and, at the same time, experienced a shortage of spiritual fruit (Gal. 5:22-23)? Circle your answer:

No, never       Maybe occasionally       More often than I'd like to admit

5. If you did not circle, "No, never," to the previous question, then I have a few other rather nosy questions (but with only the very best intentions, of course) to ask you:

a. How has serving the Lord while experiencing a shortage of spiritual fruit worked for you? What was it like? How did it feel? What were the results?

b. On the other hand, how has serving the Lord while experiencing the power and fruit of the Holy Spirit worked for you? What was that like? How did it feel? What were the results?

6. Luke 8:4-15 records the Parable of the Sower. In the first part of that passage (vs. 4-8), Jesus shares the story, and in the second part (vs. 9-15) He explains and interprets it. Use your Bible to read Luke 8:4-15, then record your answers to each question.

a. What is the seed?

b. According to this passage, what are some of the things that prevent us from receiving the seed and bearing fruit?

c. What was the only soil that bore lasting fruit, and whom does it represent?

d. How much fruit did it bear, and what kind of crop did it produce?

e. According to this parable, what does Jesus use to bear fruit in our lives?

f. How is Luke 8:15 similar to John 15:1-8 (the parable of the vine and branch)?

7. In what specific way is Jesus, the Vine, nourishing you through His Word? And in what way are you, the branch, flourishing and bearing fruit?

8. Read one final passage that I know will bless you: Psalm 92:12-15. Then record what it means to you in the space provided.

### Psalm 92:12-15

<sup></sup> ¹² *But the godly will flourish like palm trees and grow strong like the cedars of Lebanon.*
¹³ *For they are transplanted to the LORD's own house. They flourish in the courts of our God.*
¹⁴ *Even in old age they will still produce fruit; they will remain vital and green.*
¹⁵ *They will declare, "The LORD is just! He is my rock! There is no evil in him!"*

*reflect*

9. Remember how you went outside yesterday, took a few cuttings from bushes and plants, and brought them inside to remind you of John 15? Well, today, I want you to do something very similar.

   Take an old pair of scissors, and go outside again. But this time, search your yard, garden, or outdoor area for several plants that are similar to the vine in John 15. Take a cutting from one or more of the examples you find (a flower, a leafy limb from a shrub, or a small branch from a tree, etc.), bring it inside, and place your new cuttings in a vase filled with water. You may even want to create a pretty arrangement…or not. No pressure.

   Place the vase beside the dry cuttings you made yesterday. Then, take a note card, post-it, or small piece of paper, record John 15:5 on it, and prop it up beside your vase.

   Keep all of these things together in a place where you will see them often for the entire week. Memorize John 15:5, and allow the entire arrangement you've made to remind you of the truth of that verse.

# *day* 3: FRUITFUL LIVING

Today you will conclude your study of spiritual fruit. But first, get ready for...

1.  An Accountability Pop Quiz!

    Okay, now don't stress. I know the phrase "pop quiz" may bring back bad memories of that teacher who used to terrify you, but I promise that you will pass this quiz with flying colors. And here's some good news: today's quiz has only one question.

    Relax, take a deep breath, and begin your one-question quiz now.

    Question: Did you memorize Galatians 5:22-23? Circle your answer.

    > YES! I did.        No, but I am so happy this isn't high school history class.

    If you answered *yes*, high-five yourself, and record it word-for-word below.

    If you answered *no* (or if you completely forgot that memorizing Galatians 5:22-23 was part of your Week Four, Day Two homework), then let yourself off the hook for now. Open your Bible to Galatians 5:22-23, and record it word-for-word in the space above.

2.  With your pop quiz successfully behind you, please begin today's homework on the fruit of the Spirit as you:

    - Read each definition.
    - Read and observe each passage (which correlates with each specific fruit).
    - Use what you learned from the definition and scripture to complete each sentence.

a. **The first fruit of the Spirit is love.** The Greek transliteration for love is "agape," and it refers to a love that is willing to do whatever is necessary to meet the highest need of the object of love and not necessarily or always what the object wants or desires. It is the same kind of love spoken of in John 3:16, the love that God demonstrated to the world by giving His only Son. It is unconditional and sacrificial.[6]

**John 15:13**
Context: Jesus speaking to His disciples on the night of His arrest.

[13] *"There is no greater love than to lay down one's life for one's friends."*

**When I allow the Holy Spirit to produce the fruit of love in my life, I will…**

b. **The second fruit of the Spirit is joy.** The Greek transliteration for joy is "chara." It is related to the Greek "chairo" which means "to rejoice." Both of these words are rooted in another Greek word, "charis," which means grace. Therefore, both joy and rejoicing are rooted in grace.[7]

**John 15:11**
Context: Jesus speaking to His disciples on the night of His arrest.

[11] *"I have told you these things so that you will be filled with my joy. Yes, your joy will overflow!"*

**When I allow the Holy Spirit to produce the fruit of joy in my life, I will…**

c.  **The third fruit of the Spirit is peace.** The Greek transliteration is "eirene," which means peace, rest, and the absence of strife. It also is a result of God's grace.[8]

### John 16:33
Context: Jesus speaking to His disciples on the night of His arrest.

[33] *"I have told you all this so that you may have peace in me. Here on earth you will have many trials and sorrows. But take heart, because I have overcome the world."*

**When I allow the Holy Spirit to produce the fruit of peace in my life, I will...**

d.  **The fourth fruit of the Spirit is patience/longsuffering.** The Greek transliteration is "makrothumia," and it is exhibited as "self-restraint of the mind before it gives room to action or passion."[9] It describes someone who has the ability or right to avenge themselves, but chooses not to. It is also closely related to mercy.[10]

### Ephesians 4:2

[2] *Always be humble and gentle. Be patient with each other, making allowance for each other's faults because of your love.*

**When I allow the Holy Spirit to produce the fruit of patience in my life, I will...**

e. **The fifth fruit of the Spirit is kindness/gentleness (KJV).** The Greek transliteration is "chrestotes" which is associated with kindness. In some instances, it also is tied to philanthropy which is the practice of generous giving. It mellows our harshness like the aging process mellows and refines wine.[11]

### Ephesians 2:7

7   *So God can point to us in all future ages as examples of the incredible wealth of his grace and kindness toward us, as shown in all he has done for us who are united with Christ Jesus.*

**When I allow the Holy Spirit to produce the fruit of kindness in my life, I will…**

f. **The sixth fruit of the Spirit is goodness.** The Greek transliteration is "agathosune." It is something we do – it is actively exercising goodness. Although it may seem similar to "crestotes" (kindness), it is passionate not mellow. It will do whatever it takes to produce good.[12]

### Romans 15:14

14   *I am fully convinced, my dear brothers and sisters, that you are full of goodness. You know these things so well you can teach each other all about them.*

**When I allow the Holy Spirit to produce the fruit of goodness in my life, I will…**

g. **The seventh fruit of the Spirit is faithfulness/faith (KJV).** The Greek transliteration is "pistis." It describes a person whose knowledge of the truth produces confidence in the truth which, in turn, results in good works.[13]

### Luke 12:28
Context: Jesus is speaking.

[28] *"And if God cares so wonderfully for flowers that are here today and thrown into the fire tomorrow, he will certainly care for you. Why do you have so little faith?"*

**When I allow the Holy Spirit to produce the fruit of faithfulness in my life, I will…**

h. **The eighth fruit of the Spirit is gentleness/meekness (KJV).** The Greek transliteration is "praotes." It is "an inward grace of the soul, calmness toward God in particular."[14] The person who practices gentleness/meekness will accept God's will and way for them as good.[15]

### Colossians 3:12-13

[12] *Since God chose you to be the holy people he loves, you must clothe yourselves with tenderhearted mercy, kindness, humility, gentleness, and patience.*
[13] *Make allowance for each other's faults, and forgive anyone who offends you. Remember, the Lord forgave you, so you must forgive others.*

**When I allow the Holy Spirit to produce the fruit of gentleness/meekness in my life, I will…**

i. **The ninth fruit of the Spirit is self-control/temperance (KJV).** The Greek transliteration is "egkrateia," and it means just what it says: self-control.[16]

## 2 Peter 1:5-8

5   *In view of all this, make every effort to respond to God's promises. Supplement your faith with a generous provision of moral excellence, and moral excellence with knowledge,*
6   *and knowledge with self-control, and self-control with patient endurance, and patient endurance with godliness,*
7   *and godliness with brotherly affection, and brotherly affection with love for everyone.*
8   *The more you grow like this, the more productive and useful you will be in your knowledge of our Lord Jesus Christ.*

**When I allow the Holy Spirit to produce the fruit of self-control in my life, I will…**

*reflect*

3.   Conclude your study today by meditating upon what God has taught you. Ask Him to help you recognize and be sensitive and obedient to fruit-bearing opportunities.

# *day* 4: BY THIS ALL MEN WILL KNOW...

When you live in Texas, there's only one thing better than owning your own herd of cattle, and that's living next door to somebody else's cattle like Bill and I do. Of course, I'm just kidding, but we really do have the most lovely, laid-back herd of cattle living in the pasture adjacent to our property, and we get to enjoy all of the pleasures of owning cattle with absolutely none of the responsibilities.

As much as we've grown to love our next-door neighbors, however, the brand on their hide means we have no rights or claim on them. But as long as they provide us with free admission to their soothing sounds and rural ambience, we will continue to enjoy the blessings of their presence.

As disciples, you and I belong to Jesus. He bought and paid for us with His blood, and the scars He bears upon His body reveal His unconditional, sacrificial love for us.

What mark—what brand—do we bear that proves we belong to Jesus? Is there any visible characteristic about us that will cause others to recognize that He owns us?

The answer, of course, is yes! Today and tomorrow you will discover the "brand" that enables not only some but *all* men to know that we belong to Jesus and that we truly are disciples.

1. Begin your study today by discovering Distinctive #6 of the Devoted Disciple. Read John 13:34-35, and underline the distinguishing mark that is proof of true discipleship.

### John 13:34-35

<sup></sup> 34 *"So now I am giving you a new commandment: Love each other. Just as I have loved you, you should love each other.*
35 *Your love for one another will prove to the world that you are my disciples."*

2. In yesterday's homework, you learned the definition of love as it relates to the fruit of the Spirit. But in John 13:34, the word "love" (used three times) is slightly different. The Greek transliteration is "agapao," and it means love that is an act of the will. How does this differ from the way love is usually defined in today's culture?

3. The word "love" in John 13:35 is "agape," the same word used in Galatians 5:22 to describe the first fruit of the Spirit. Take a moment to review that definition by turning to your Day Three homework, Question 2a. Then record in your own words what Jesus was teaching His disciples in John 13:34-35.

4. As you think about all that you've studied about the Casual Christians in 1 Corinthians, would they meet the standard Jesus set in John 13:34-35 for loving one another? Circle your answer.

   Yes          No

   John 13:34-35 and 1 Corinthians 1-3 reveal Distinctive #6 of Devoted Disciples and Casual Christians:

   | DEVOTED DISCIPLE | CASUAL CHRISTIAN |
   |---|---|
   | Distinctive # 6: Unconditional love for others. *—John 13:34-35* | Distinctive # 6: Conditional love for others. *—1 Cor. 1-3* |

5. What did Jesus mean in John 13:34 when He said, "I am giving you a new commandment: Love each other. Just as I have loved you, you should love each other"? Use your Bible to read the following scripture, and answer each question.

   a. Leviticus 19:18—What is the command regarding love in this verse?

   b. How is Jesus' command in John 13:34 "new" or different from the command in Leviticus 19:18?

c.  What example did Jesus use to help them understand this new commandment?

6.  In Day One and Two of your homework, you studied John 15:1-8. Now I want you to see the larger context of that passage and how it relates to the "new commandment" Jesus spoke of in John 13. Use your Bible to read John 15:1-17. Then record a list of any new insights you learn about love and how to love like Jesus.

*reflect*

7.  How is your "love life?" Respond to what Jesus has taught you today about loving others by spending time with Him now in prayer and by praying for all of the "others" in your life.

*day 5:* LOVE IS...

You've had a very full week of study, precious sister, so today's homework will be brief. Your focus will be on Distinctive #6 of Devoted Disciples: Unconditional love for others.

1. It is no accident that one of the greatest passages in the entire Bible on love is found in a letter written to a group of Casual Christians who were struggling to demonstrate love to one other. And although I realize that you are probably very familiar with 1 Corinthians 13, I want you to read it twice today.

As you read through it the first time, draw a heart around the word "love" each time you read it. Then slowly and carefully read and observe the entire chapter a second time. As you read, make notes in the space below the passage of any insights and application the Holy Spirit reveals to you.

### 1 Corinthians 13:1-13

1. *If I could speak all the languages of earth and of angels, but didn't love others, I would only be a noisy gong or a clanging cymbal.*

2. *If I had the gift of prophecy, and if I understood all of God's secret plans and possessed all knowledge, and if I had such faith that I could move mountains, but didn't love others, I would be nothing.*

3. *If I gave everything I have to the poor and even sacrificed my body, I could boast about it; but if I didn't love others, I would have gained nothing.*

4. *Love is patient and kind. Love is not jealous or boastful or proud*

5. *or rude. It does not demand its own way. It is not irritable, and it keeps no record of being wronged.*

6. *It does not rejoice about injustice but rejoices whenever the truth wins out.*

7. *Love never gives up, never loses faith, is always hopeful, and endures through every circumstance.*

8. *Prophecy and speaking in unknown languages and special knowledge will become useless. But love will last forever!*

9. *Now our knowledge is partial and incomplete, and even the gift of prophecy reveals only part of the whole picture!*

10. *But when full understanding comes, these partial things will become useless.*

11. *When I was a child, I spoke and thought and reasoned as a child. But when I grew up, I put away childish things.*

12. *Now we see things imperfectly as in a cloudy mirror, but then we will see everything with perfect clarity. All that I know now is partial and incomplete, but then I will know everything completely, just as God now knows me completely.*

13. *Three things will last forever—faith, hope, and love—and the greatest of these is love.*

*reflect*

2. Conclude your study this week by completing this prayer: Jesus, I praise and thank you today for all that You have taught and shown me this week. But I thank you most of all for teaching and showing me that...

*Discipleship is tested not by the creed you recite, not by the hymns you sing, not by the ritual you observe, but by the fact that you love one another. The measure in which Christians love one another is the measure in which the world believes in them or their Christ. It is the final test of discipleship.*

—Henrietta C Mears, *What the Bible is All About*[17]

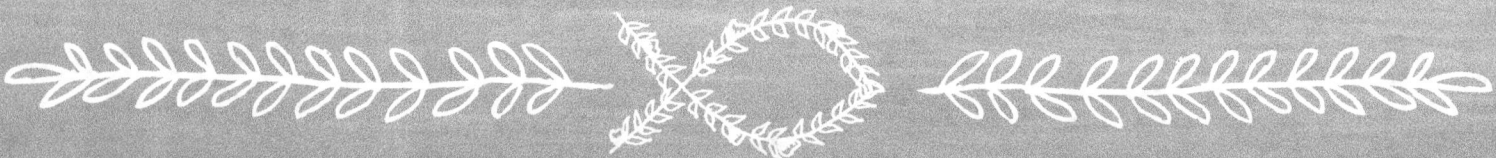

# An FAQ for Disciples Re: Fruit & Love

1. **Why is bearing fruit necessary?** It _____ God and _____ that you are a _____. *John 15:8*

2. **How do you bear fruit?** You abide in the _____ _____/_____ _____. *John 15:1, 4*

3. **How do you know if you are abiding?**

    a. You will _____ _____.
    b. You will be _____.
    c. You will experience _____ _____. *John 15:7*

4. **What kind of fruit will you bear?**

    a. Others will be _____. *John 4:35–36*
    b. Spiritual growth/_____. *Rom. 6:22*
    c. _____. *Rom. 15:28*
    d. _____ of the _____. *Gal. 5:22-23*
    e. Good _____. *Col. 1:10*
    f. _____ and _____ to God. *Heb. 13:15*

5. **How does God prune you?**

    a. Through His _____. *John 15:3, 2 Tim. 3:16-17*
    b. Through His _____. *Heb. 12:6, Ps. 119:67*

6. **Why does God prune you?** So you will _____ _____ _____. *John 15:2*

7. **Why is loving one another necessary?** It _____ God and _____ that you are a _____. *John 13:35*

8. **Who are you required to love?**

    a. _____. *Matt. 22:37*
    b. One another/_____ _____. *John 13:35*
    c. Your neighbors/_____. *Matt. 19:19*
    d. Your _____. *Matt. 5:44*
       = _____.

9. **How do you demonstrate love?**

    a. _____. *John 14:15*
    b. _____. *John 15:12-13, John 3:16, 1 John 3:16*

are you a DISCIPLE?

# week 6

# DEVOTED DISCIPLE: DISTINCTIVE 7

*Be imitators of me, just as I also am of Christ.*
— 1 Corinthians 11:1 (NASB)

# *day 1:* TRUTHFULNESS & COMPASSION

They say, "opposites attract," but "they" have never met my husband, Bill, and his sister, Cyndi. From the stories I have heard about their childhood and teenage years, their personalities were as different as night and day. It's a wonder they both survived.

Cyndi and I got to know one another when we were college roommates, and two years later we became sisters-in-law. Today, I am happy to report, Bill and Cyndi share a very strong bond of mutual love and respect for one another (due in large part because they have both matured and, okay, probably also because they no longer live under the same roof).

Long before their rivalry ended, however, I noticed that, as different as Bill and Cindy were, they still shared a very similar style of communication: they were both straight shooters. They were honest, forthright, direct, and no-holds-barred. Not rude. Not disrespectful. Both siblings simply speak their mind and never mind what others think. They are truth tellers.

As much as I admire and appreciate a straight shooter and a truth teller, I struggle at times to be one. Not because I don't tell the truth…I just don't always want to tell the hard part of the truth. The part that might upset or offend someone. And sometimes (not always, which is why we must be very careful and very sensitive to the Holy Spirit) Jesus wants us to tell the whole truth even if it upsets or offends.

Precious sister, there is a fine line between truth telling and compassion, and Jesus can teach us how to do both. This week you will study seven aspects of Christlike character and, just like truth-telling and compassion, some of them may seem very opposite from one another—kind of like Bill and Cyndi.

As Christians, we are all very different, and following Jesus will never make all of our differences disappear. However, following Jesus *will* lead us toward the same goal: to become imitators of Christ.

1. Begin your study today by discovering Distinctive #7 of the Devoted Disciple and the Casual Christian. Read the descriptions in the boxes below. Then use your Bible to look up the verse corresponding to each description (Luke 6:40, 1 Cor. 3:3). Record each verse word-for-word in the space provided under each description.

| DEVOTED DISCIPLE | CASUAL CHRISTIAN |
|---|---|
| Distinctive # 7: Christlike character. —*Luke 6:40* | Distinctive # 7: Worldly character. —*1 Cor. 3:3* |

_____

_____

_____

2. The first characteristic of Christlike behavior that you will study is **Truthfulness**. Use your Bible to read the following passages that describe conversations Jesus had with two very different people. Then record your insights noting:

- What you learn about Nicodemus and the Samaritan woman.
- What you learn about each of their backgrounds.
- How Jesus responds to them.
- How Jesus treats them.
- Specific characteristics Jesus exhibits.
- What you learn about truthfulness.

a. John 3:1-22

    b.  John 4:1-42

Depending upon your personality, some of the characteristics of Christlike behavior may be easier for you to develop than others. But what I hope you will see in this week's homework is how vital each of these characteristics is.

For instance, what if Jesus had been afraid of offending Nicodemus? What if He had been less than truthful with the Samaritan woman? Because Jesus wasn't afraid to confront them with the truth, they believed in Him, received salvation, and were able to point others to Christ (see John 19:39 for more information pointing to Nicodemus' conversion).

As disciples, Jesus is going to give us opportunities to share the gospel in conversations we have with others. When He does, we must follow His lead and be truthful.

3.   The second characteristic of Christlike behavior is **Compassion**. Use your Bible to read the following passages, then record your answers to the questions and what you learn from Jesus about compassion.

    a.  Matthew 9:35-38 – Why did Jesus feel compassion, and what instruction did He give to His disciples?

    b.  Matthew 20:29-34 – Describe who the "multitude" likely was. What characteristics did they exhibit? What did Jesus teach them that day?

c.  Luke 7:11-17 – Describe the scene. Did anyone ask Jesus to do what He did, and what does this teach you about showing compassion? What was the result of Jesus' compassion?

d.  Luke 10:29-37 – Why did Jesus share this story, and what is His command to us today?

*reflect*

4.  Conclude your study today by prayerfully asking the Holy Spirit to reveal the truthfulness and compassion level in your own life. Score yourself on the scale below. Finally, record the names of those to whom Jesus wants you to demonstrate truthfulness and compassion, then pray for them and prepare your heart to obey Him.

On a scale of 1-5 (1 being the lowest and 5 the highest), circle the number that most closely represents your:

Level of Truthfulness        1        2        3        4        5

Level of Compassion          1        2        3        4        5

# *day 2:* MEEKNESS & BOLDNESS

Yesterday, you began studying **Distinctive #7 of the Devoted Disciple: Christlike Character**. You also learned the first two characteristics: **Truthfulness** and **Compassion**. These two very opposite attributes create a perfect blend.

Today and tomorrow you will study two more seemingly opposite characteristics: **Meekness** and **Boldness**. Begin today's homework by learning what "meekness" means. It may just surprise you.

1. Some of my favorite Bible study tools were written by Dr. Spiros Zodhiates, a godly Greek-American scholar and theologian whose life's work made it possible for non-scholars like me to understand the original Hebrew (Old Testament) and Greek (New Testament) languages of the Bible. Although Dr. Zodhiates is in heaven now, isn't it beautiful how God continues to use him to help us today?

   I used to think meekness meant weakness but, as you are about to see, nothing could be farther from the truth. Read the following definition and, as you read, ask God to help you become a living, breathing definition of meekness:

   > Meekness is an inwrought grace of the soul, and the expressions of it are primarily toward God. It is that attitude of spirit [in which] we accept God's dealing with us as good and do not dispute or resist. …[Meekness] is getting angry at the right time, in the right measure, and for the right reason. …It is a condition of the mind and heart which demonstrates gentleness, not in weakness, but in power. It is a balance born in strength of character.[1]

2. As you review the definition of meekness, are there any circumstances in your life right now that are causing you to question the way God is dealing with you or someone you love? Record your answer.

3. **Meekness** and **Boldness** go hand in hand. Use your Bible to read the following passages, then record your answers to these questions regarding each passage:

- How does this passage reveal the meekness as well as the boldness of Christ?
- What instructions does Jesus teach regarding these characteristics?

a. Matthew 11:20-30

b. Matthew 18:1-6

c. Matthew 23:1-12

d. John 10:1-18

*reflect*

4. As you conclude your time in God's Word today, take a few minutes to journal your own thoughts concerning how God may be speaking to you about your current circumstances (or the circumstances of someone you love). Then complete the sentence below:

Dear Lord, in light of what You've shown me today, I believe you want me to view and respond to my circumstances by…

_____

_____

_____

_____

# *day 3:* MEEKNESS & BOLDNESS—ESSENTIALS FOR CONFLICT

I hate conflict, but I hate confronting conflict even more, especially conflict between Christians.

From what I have witnessed in my own 50+ years of church involvement, these are the top three causes for conflict between brothers and sisters in Christ:

1) **Sin**—Example: Someone loses their temper, gets jealous, or becomes involved in an adulterous relationship, and conflict ensues.

2) **A decision made**—Example: A church program or class is added or cut, people take sides, and division and disunity erupt.

3) **A personality clash**—Example: Two very opposite people disagree on a non-essential church issue which leads to a severing of fellowship and a broken relationship.

Precious sister, even if you hate conflict and confronting conflict as much as I do, there will be times when you and I must step up to the plate and do our part in order to bring about reconciliation and restoration. When we do, **meekness** is an absolute essential.

Conflict will also come our way from the world and its opposition to everything we believe. As disciples of Jesus, **boldness** will be required on our part.

Today, you will continue your study of the Christlike characteristics of meekness and boldness. Study well because, I promise, conflict is coming, and disciples are not immune to conflict (check out Paul and Barnabas in Acts 15:36-41).

**Christlike character: It is not for wimps.** But it is for those who are disciples.

1. Review quickly the definition of "meekness" that was included in yesterday's homework. How will meekness enable you to handle conflict?

2. Read the following passages (I have included two translations so that you will not miss the reference to meekness). Then record what you learn about when, why, and how to practice meekness and any other insights you glean.

### a. Galatians 6:1 (KJV)

> ¹ Brethren, if a man be overtaken in a fault, ye which are spiritual, restore such an one in the spirit of meekness; considering thyself, lest thou also be tempted.

### Galatians 6:1 (NLT)

> ¹ Dear brothers and sisters, if another believer is overcome by some sin, you who are godly should gently and humbly help that person back onto the right path. And be careful not to fall into the same temptation yourself.

### b. 1 Peter 3:1-4 (KJV)

> ¹ Likewise, ye wives, be in subjection to your own husbands; that, if any obey not the word, they also may without the word be won by the conversation of the wives;
> ² While they behold your chaste conversation coupled with fear.
> ³ Whose adorning let it not be that outward adorning of plaiting the hair, and of wearing of gold, or of putting on of apparel;
> ⁴ But let it be the hidden man of the heart, in that which is not corruptible, even the ornament of a meek and quiet spirit, which is in the sight of God of great price.

### 1 Peter 3:1-4 (NLT)

> ¹ In the same way, you wives must accept the authority of your husbands. Then, even if some refuse to obey the Good News, your godly lives will speak to them without any words. They will be won over
> ² by observing your pure and reverent lives.
> ³ Don't be concerned about the outward beauty of fancy hairstyles, expensive jewelry, or beautiful clothes.
> ⁴ You should clothe yourselves instead with the beauty that comes from within, the unfading beauty of a gentle and quiet spirit, which is so precious to God.

c. The word "meekness" is not used in this passage, but because it does include Jesus' instructions regarding conflict, I am including it. Also, when it comes to conflict, it is always wise to exercise meekness.

### Matthew 18:15-17 (NLT)

15 "If another believer sins against you, go privately and point out the offense. If the other person listens and confesses it, you have won that person back.

16 But if you are unsuccessful, take one or two others with you and go back again, so that everything you say may be confirmed by two or three witnesses.

17 If the person still refuses to listen, take your case to the church. Then if he or she won't accept the church's decision, treat that person as a pagan or a corrupt tax collector."

d. One more passage that I want you to study is 1 Thessalonians 5:12-15. The word "meekness" is not used in this passage either, but it is a wonderful passage of instruction to the church regarding avoiding conflict and dealing with it in the right spirit—and meekness is always the right spirit.

### 1 Thessalonians 5:12-15 (NLT)

12 Dear brothers and sisters, honor those who are your leaders in the Lord's work. They work hard among you and give you spiritual guidance.

13 Show them great respect and wholehearted love because of their work. And live peacefully with each other.

14 Brothers and sisters, we urge you to warn those who are lazy. Encourage those who are timid. Take tender care of those who are weak. Be patient with everyone.

15 See that no one pays back evil for evil, but always try to do good to each other and to all people.

3. Before you begin your study on boldness, open your Bible to Ephesians 4:25-27. What does this passage teach regarding conflict between Christians, and how does it relate to meekness?

4. Are you experiencing conflict with another Christian—a family member, relative, friend, or church member? According to what you've just studied, what would Jesus have you do?

5. Complete your study today by reading the following passages and recording what you learn about how and when to practice the Christlike characteristic of boldness and any other insights you glean.

   a. Acts 4:13 (Be sure to note the context; also, the word "confidence" may be used instead of "boldness" in your Bible.)

   b. Acts 4:29-31(Again, please note the context.)

   c. Acts 14:1-3

   d. Acts 19:8-10

*reflect*

6. What opportunities is God giving you today to be bold in your faith? Record your answer, then make Paul's prayer request to the believers at Ephesus your own by spending a few moments in prayer.

*And pray for me, too. Ask God to give me the right words so I can boldly explain God's mysterious plan that the Good News is for Jews and Gentiles alike.*

— Ephesians 6:19

P.S. Today's study has focused on exercising meekness and boldness in the church and in public. But both of these Christlike characteristics can be applied to many other areas of your life. If you have children and teenagers, I'm especially talking to you, Mom. ☺

## *day 4*: MERCY & FORGIVENESS

Before you begin today's study on the Christlike Characteristics of **Mercy** and **Forgiveness**…

Before you begin to think even once, "But, Lord, surely you're not saying that I have to show mercy and forgiveness to _____ (fill in the blank with someone who has hurt you)."

Before you convince yourself that you cannot do today's homework because of the emotions and past traumas it may cause you to recall, I want you to read this:

**1 Peter 2:21-24**

21 *For God called you to do good, even if it means suffering, just as Christ suffered for you. He is your example, and you must follow in his steps.*

22 *He never sinned, nor ever deceived anyone.*

23 *He did not retaliate when he was insulted, nor threaten revenge when he suffered. He left his case in the hands of God, who always judges fairly.*

24 *He personally carried our sins in his body on the cross so that we can be dead to sin and live for what is right. By his wounds you are healed.*

When you think about the suffering Jesus experienced for your sake…

When you think about the mercy He extended from His nail-pierced hands and feet…

When you think about the forgiveness His blood paid for your sin…

You must follow His example, and in His steps live every day.

Precious sister, this may be a difficult day of study for you, but Jesus did the most difficult thing anyone has ever done for you. Now He is calling you to, "Follow Me."

1. As you continue your study of **Distinctive #7 of the Devoted Disciple: Christlike Character**, begin today's homework by reading the descriptions of **Mercy** and **Forgiveness**. As you read, ask God to help you express the same kind of mercy and forgiveness to others that He has expressed to you through His Son.

   a. **Mercy** as defined in the Bible means to show mercy, to extend help for the consequences of sin, and to be gracious. Mercy is active, benevolent compassion involving both thought and action.[2]

   b. **Forgiveness** as defined in the Bible means granting pardon, being gracious to others, and to cancel a debt. The root of this word is *charis* which is the Greek word for "grace," and grace is a favor done without expectation of return; it is unearned, unmerited favor.[3]

2. Use what you just learned to complete the following sentences in your own words:

   a. **When I demonstrate the Christlike character of mercy to someone, I will…**

   b. **When I demonstrate the Christlike character of forgiveness to someone, I will…**

3. Circle your answers to the following questions:

   a. Have you demonstrated mercy or forgiveness to someone recently?

      Yes          No

   b. Have you withheld mercy or forgiveness from someone recently or in your past?

      Yes          No

4. What did Jesus teach and demonstrate about mercy? Read the following scriptures, and record your answer.

   a. Matthew 5:7

   b. Matthew 9:27-30

   c. Matthew 18:21-35

5. Discover what Jesus taught about forgiveness. Read the following passages, and record what you learn.

   a. Matthew 6:12-15

b. Mark 11:25-26

c. Luke 23:34

6. There is one final passage I want you to read before you complete today's homework. As you read it, rejoice and thank God for His mercy and forgiveness to you:

**Ephesians 2:4-7**

4   But God is so rich in mercy, and he loved us so much,
5   that even though we were dead because of our sins, he gave us life when he raised Christ from the dead. (It is only by God's grace that you have been saved!)
6   For he raised us from the dead along with Christ and seated us with him in the heavenly realms because we are united with Christ Jesus.
7   So God can point to us in all future ages as examples of the incredible wealth of his grace and kindness toward us, as shown in all he has done for us who are united with Christ Jesus.

*reflect*

7. Forgiveness is an act of mercy. So, before you can forgive, you must first extend mercy; then forgiveness follows. How can this help you forgive those who have hurt or harmed you? Record your answer.

One more thing: If you circled "yes" to Question 3b, will you demonstrate Christlike character toward that person(s) by exercising mercy and forgiveness now? Circle your answer:

Yes       No

P. S. If someone is aware of your lack of mercy and forgiveness toward them, go to them, pick up the phone and call them, or send them a note. Humbly express your desire to forgive (and be forgiven if you have hurt them by withholding forgiveness) by extending mercy and forgiveness to them. Be free! Live out the truth you have learned today.

# *day 5:* SERVANTHOOD

Perhaps you're wondering why I didn't include love, joy, and many other attributes in this week's study of Christlike character. There are two reasons:

1) You studied the fruit of the Spirit—which includes love, joy, peace, etc.—in last week's lesson, and Jesus, of course, possesses them all.

2) When I think about the attributes of Christ, I feel just like the Apostle John must have felt when he wrote, "Jesus also did many other things. If they were all written down, I suppose the whole world could not contain the books that would be written" (John 21:25). One 8-week Bible study could never begin to contain all of the characteristics of Christ.

Today, your study will be light (you like that, don't you?). As you study the Christlike characteristic of **Servanthood**, be prepared to practice it very soon.

If you're like most women I know, you've been practicing servanthood for years. May the Divine Servant encourage you today to follow Him as both a disciple and a servant.

1. Use your Bible to read John 13:1-17. As you read it, visualize the scene in that Upper Room in your mind. After you've read the entire passage, answer the following questions:

   a. What motivated Jesus to be a servant (v. 1), and what can you learn from Him concerning your own motivation to serve?

   b. What did Jesus know that night as He took up the towel and washed the disciples' feet (vs. 1 & 3)?

c.  If you've ever felt like a Mommy Martyr, a Teacher Martyr, an Office Martyr, or any other kind of martyr, what is Jesus teaching you about servanthood?

d.  As He washed Judas' feet, what is Jesus teaching you about servanthood?

e.  What was Jesus' primary purpose in washing the disciples' feet (v. 12-15)?

*reflect*

2.  Last week I asked you to create an arrangement to symbolize John 15:1-8 to remind you of the truths contained in that passage. Today, I want you to do something similar in hopes that it will remind you to be a servant just like Jesus was.

    Go to your kitchen, pull a dish towel out of a drawer, and throw it over your shoulder (like those good ol' Southern cooks used to do). Or, if you prefer, fold the towel in half lengthwise, and tuck it into your waistband. Wear that dish towel as long as possible today (you may want to begin doing this every day).

    Let that dish towel remind you of what Jesus did as He "wrapped a towel around His waist" (John 13:4), washed the disciples' feet, and said to them, to you, and to me:

    *"You call me 'Teacher' and 'Lord,' and you are right, because that's what I am. And since I, your Lord and Teacher, have washed your feet, you ought to wash each other's feet. I have given you an example to follow. Do as I have done to you. I tell you the truth, slaves are not greater than their master. Nor is the messenger more important than the one who sends the message. Now that you know these things, God will bless you for doing them."*

    — John 13:13-17

Precious sister, serve Him as you serve others!

*You also became imitators of us and of the Lord.*
— 1 Thessalonians 1:6 (NASB)

are you a DISCIPLE?

# Christlike Character: Real Disciples & Role Models

1. Truthfulness: Ex. _____ *1 Cor. 1:10-13, 3:1-4, 4:14-16*

2. Compassion: Ex. _____ *Luke 10:33-34, Luke 15:20, Col. 4:14, Philem. 1:23-24, 2 Tim. 4:11*

3. Meekness: Ex. _____ *Luke 3:16, John 3:22-30*

4. Boldness: Ex. _____ *Acts 4:18-20, 5:27-32*

5. Mercy: Ex. _____ *Acts 9:26-27, 15:36-40, 2 Tim. 2:11*

6. Forgiveness: Ex. _____ *Acts 6:8-15, Acts 7:57-60*

7. Servanthood: Ex. _____ *Mark 14:3-9, Luke 6:40*

are you a DISCIPLE?

148

# week 7

## DISCIPLES MAKE DISCIPLES

*"I [Jesus] tell you the truth, anyone who believes in me will do the same works I have done, and even greater works, because I am going to be with the Father."*

— John 14:12

# day 1: AS YOU GO, MAKE DISCIPLES

Once upon a time fifty years ago, there was an enormous tent filled with rows and rows of hard metal folding chairs all facing a simple stage. Streams of people arrived every evening filling every chair. Revival had come, word had spread, and everyone in town had heard about what God was doing inside that tent each night.

With my six-year-old legs dangling from the much-too-big metal chair, I remember sitting under that tent beside Mother one evening while Daddy was on the stage. As the piano and organ played, Daddy led the choir and congregation in singing. He paved the way through his solo for the evangelist to preach the gospel and draw the net.

When the message ended and the invitation was given, I left my seat, walked up the aisle to the front, and gave my heart and life to Jesus. It was and still is the best decision I have ever made in all of my 56 years.

I told you about that decision on the very first day of this study. I also told you that it wasn't until many years later that I became a disciple. What I didn't tell you, however, is what happened in my life during the years between my salvation decision (at six) and my disciple decision (at 22). To sum it up, God graciously and faithfully discipled me.[1]

As the daughter of an evangelist, God gave me the privilege of attending dozens of revivals and Bible conferences where I sat under some of His finest preachers—some of whose sermons I remember to this day. And because our family was active in our local church, God used pastors, Sunday School teachers, youth ministers, volunteers, and individual church members to both shape and instruct me through the Word and through their examples. However, the greatest role models and examples God used to teach me what following Jesus really meant were my own parents.

Although I didn't understand it then, I now know that all of those experiences and all of those people were preparing me to become a disciple. They also were preparing me to do what they had done: to disciple others.

Becoming a disciple of Jesus Christ is Step One in the discipleship process. Step Two is making disciples.

Who has God used to disciple you? And who has He called *you* to disciple?

Precious sister, if you've taken Step One (and I pray that you have), it's time to take Step Two because Jesus commands you to become a disciple who makes disciples.

1. After His resurrection, Jesus appeared to the disciples and instructed them for forty days (Acts 1:3). His final instruction before His ascension is called the Great Commission, and it is included in all four of The Gospels and the Book of Acts (Matt. 28:19-20, Mark 16:15, Luke 24:47, John 20:21, and Acts 1:8). Find Matthew 28:19-20 in your Bible, and record it word-for-word in the space provided.

2. According to Jesus, what is your mission and what does it involve?

3. What promise does Jesus give you as you fulfill your mission?

4. Read what Jesus promised the disciples in John 14:16-18, 26. How does this explain and parallel His promise in Matthew 28:20?

One of the side effects of being the daughter of an evangelist and attending so many evangelistic meetings when I was young is that I was exposed to the Great Commission. Frequently. The word "go" was often emphasized as the primary command of Matthew 28:19-20, and the most frequently used Bible translation of that day and time (the *King James Version*) translated the passage like this:

## Matthew 28:19-20 (KJV)

¹⁹ *"Go ye therefore, and teach all nations, baptizing them in the name of the Father, and of the Son, and of the Holy Ghost:*

²⁰ *Teaching them to observe all things whatsoever I have commanded you: and, lo, I am with you alway, even unto the end of the world. Amen."*

Somewhere in all of that evangelistic, *King James Version* teaching, I got the distinct impression that my primary mission as a believer was to go, GO, **GO** and teach the gospel to unbelievers. I believed that my #1 responsibility, according to the Great Commission, was to be an evangelist. And if there was one thing I knew from being around evangelists all the time it was this: I was *not* an evangelist.

Many years later, through the discipleship training I received from Precept® Ministries, I learned the truth that set me free regarding the Great Commission. Turns out, when you study the original Greek language and verb tenses in Matthew 28:19-20, the word "go" is not the primary command. Also, the word "teach" is best translated "make disciples," and "make disciples" *is* the primary command of the Great Commission.

Warren Wiersbe, a wonderful Bible scholar and theologian, explains Matthew 28:19-20 like this: "The only command in the entire Great Commission is "make disciples" ("teach all nations"). Jesus said, 'While you are going, make disciples of all the nations.'"[2] Wiersbe also is careful to say this, however: "No matter where we are, we should be witnesses for Jesus Christ and seek to win others to Him (Acts 11:19-21)."[3]

As Jesus' disciples, we won't all be evangelists. But as we go about our day-to-day lives, we will all be witnesses as we share our faith with others, and we must all make disciples.

5. The final aspect you will study today about the Great Commission isn't included in Matthew 28:19-20, but it is included in Acts 1:8 (a verse you studied in Week Four). Read it below, then answer the questions that follow.

### Acts 1:8 (NASB)

⁸ *"But you will receive power when the Holy Spirit has come upon you; and you shall be My witnesses both in Jerusalem, and in all Judea and Samaria, and even to the remotest part of the earth."*

a. What will the power of the Holy Spirit enable you to do?

b. Where did Jesus command those very first disciples to be His witnesses?

c. If you have a Bible that includes a map of Israel during the time of Christ (maps are usually found in the back of your Bible), locate the specific places Jesus referred to in Acts 1:8. If your Bible doesn't include maps, go online and search "map of Israel during the time of Christ." Your search will soon lead you to a map where you can locate the specific places of which Jesus spoke.

d. Where were the disciples when Jesus commissioned them in Acts 1:8, and where did they go after Jesus' ascension? To find the answer, read Acts 1:12.

e. Were they witnesses in Jerusalem? Quickly scan Acts 2:1-41, then circle your answer.

   Yes          No

f. Were they witnesses in Judea? Read Acts 8:1-5, then circle your answer.

   Yes          No

6. Acts 10-28 records how the disciples obeyed the Great Commission and made disciples even in the most remote places. Today, Jesus calls us to be His witnesses. How can we obey the Great Commission? Where is your Jerusalem, Judea, Samaria, and how can you be a witness to even the remotest parts of the earth? Think about these questions, and record your insights.

*reflect*

7. As you reflect upon what you have studied today, how is Jesus calling you to take the first step of Step Two and make disciples? Record your answer.

_____

_____

_____

_____

_____

_____

# *day 2:* HOW DISCIPLES MAKE DISCIPLES

Yesterday you studied the last words Jesus spoke on His last day on earth. Until He returns to earth once more (Rev. 19:11), Jesus' final words are our mission and goal. His primary purpose for placing us here on the earth at this specific time in history is so that we will glorify Him by making disciples.

Soooo…how do you actually make disciples?

Very simply, you do what Jesus did. You form relationships with others who want to follow Christ. You share with them what Jesus has taught you. You do the ups and downs of life with them, and you allow them to observe your own relationship with God and others through those ups and downs. You encourage and challenge them and, most of all, you demonstrate the power and love of Christ to them.

One of the best examples of disciples making disciples is found in 1 Thessalonians. The Christians at the church in Thessalonica faced many of the same cultural obstacles we face today. Yet, in spite of their idolatrous and worldly environment, God used the church at Thessalonica to make disciples far beyond their borders.

As you study the example of the church at Thessalonica, may you be encouraged to follow their example and become a disciple who makes disciples.

1. Get to know the back story of the church at Thessalonica by reading Acts 17:1-10. Record a brief summary of how they came to Christ and the circumstances they faced because of their newfound faith.

2. Now read the first chapter of Paul's first letter to the church at Thessalonica. But don't just read it once; read and observe it carefully several times. In the margins, record your insights regarding:

- Their witness
- Any distinctives of Devoted Disciples they exhibit
- How they responded to the Great Commission
- How they made disciples
- Any insights or encouragement you gain from their example

### 1 Thessalonians 1:1-10

¹ *This letter is from Paul, Silas, and Timothy. We are writing to the church in Thessalonica, to you who belong to God the Father and the Lord Jesus Christ. May God give you grace and peace.*

² *We always thank God for all of you and pray for you constantly.*

³ *As we pray to our God and Father about you, we think of your faithful work, your loving deeds, and the enduring hope you have because of our Lord Jesus Christ.*

⁴ *We know, dear brothers and sisters, that God loves you and has chosen you to be his own people.*

⁵ *For when we brought you the Good News, it was not only with words but also with power, for the Holy Spirit gave you full assurance that what we said was true. And you know of our concern for you from the way we lived when we were with you.*

⁶ *So you received the message with joy from the Holy Spirit in spite of the severe suffering it brought you. In this way, you imitated both us and the Lord.*

⁷ *As a result, you have become an example to all the believers in Greece—throughout both Macedonia and Achaia.*

⁸ *And now the word of the Lord is ringing out from you to people everywhere, even beyond Macedonia and Achaia, for wherever we go we find people telling us about your faith in God. We don't need to tell them about it,*

⁹ *for they keep talking about the wonderful welcome you gave us and how you turned away from idols to serve the living and true God.*

¹⁰ *And they speak of how you are looking forward to the coming of God's Son from heaven—Jesus, whom God raised from the dead. He is the one who has rescued us from the terrors of the coming judgment.*

Are you ready to join the Church at Thessalonica? I hope you already have by joining and actively serving in a Bible-believing, disciple-making, evangelistic local church in your area. According to the model Jesus set with His group of twelve disciples and the others who followed with them, and according the model of the New Testament church as seen in Acts through Revelation, it is absolutely essential that you be connected with a body of believers—a church.

But don't just take it from me. Look what the writer of Hebrews says:

**Hebrews 10:24-25**

*24  Let us think of ways to motivate one another to acts of love and good works.*
*25  And let us not neglect our meeting together, as some people do, but encourage one another, especially now that the day of his return is drawing near.*

*reflect*

3.  First Thessalonians 1:7 describes the believers at Thessalonica as "an example to all the believers." What opportunities is God giving you to be "an example to all the believers?" Who is observing your life and example? How are you serving currently in a local church? Record your answers.

_____

_____

_____

_____

_____

_____

_____

_____

_____

# *day 3:* THE REALITIES & REWARDS OF BEING A DISCIPLE

You probably noticed in your study of the church at Thessalonica yesterday that being a disciple doesn't mean that God will give you a hall pass so you can skip suffering. As you learned way back in Week Two, the cost of discipleship involves taking up your cross daily to follow Christ (Luke 9:23).

Today you will study the hard reality that every true disciple will face: persecution. But you will also discover the sweet reward Jesus promises all who follow Him.

1. Read each of the following passages and record what you learn about persecution and suffering, and how to respond to them.

   a. Matthew 10:23

   b. John 15:18-21

   c. John 17:14

2. Now take a look at suffering and persecution from a different perspective. Read the following passages and record what you learn about suffering and persecution.

   a. Luke 6:22-23

   b. 2 Corinthians 1:5-10

   c. Philippians 1:29

   d. 1 Peter 1:6-7

3. What are the rewards of discipleship? Using your Bible, read the following passages and record what you learn:

    a.  Matthew 10:42

    b.  Luke 12:8

    c.  John 14:21-23

    d.  Revelation 21:1-4

    e.  Revelation 22:3-5

Can you say *Glory?!* Yes, discipleship will include trials, suffering, and even persecution, but I trust you have seen that the rewards far outweigh them all.

*reflect*

4.  What about you? Are you suffering or experiencing persecution? How did God speak to you through His Word today? How can suffering enhance your faith? Record your answer, then spend a few moments in prayer praising and thanking Him for the blessings and rewards He gives to those who belong to Him even when they suffer.

_____

_____

_____

_____

_____

## *days* 4&5: WHAT HAS JESUS TAUGHT YOU?

On these final two days of your study, I think it is very important for you to review what Jesus has taught you over the past seven weeks. My goal and prayer in asking you to do this is that it will cement the primary truths you have learned through His Word into your heart and mind.

1.  Your assignment is to compile a list of the top two truths, principles, or instructions you have learned. But that's not all because, as you know, knowledge is one thing; doing is another (James 1:22). The second part of your assignment is to record what you will do with the knowledge Jesus has taught you.

    Today you will review Weeks 1-3. Tomorrow you will review Weeks 4-7. As you review (and please don't rush), use the following charts to record what Jesus has taught you and how you will obey Him.

## The Top 2 Truths Jesus Has Taught Me About Discipleship

### Week One

*The top two things Jesus taught me were…*

*I will follow, obey, and practice what He's taught me by…*

**The Top 2 Truths Jesus Has Taught Me About Discipleship**

**Week Two**

*The top two things Jesus taught me were…*

*I will follow, obey, and practice what He's taught me by…*

**The Top 2 Truths Jesus Has Taught Me About Discipleship**

**Week Three**

*The top two things Jesus taught me were…*

*I will follow, obey, and practice what He's taught me by…*

**The Top 2 Truths Jesus Has Taught Me About Discipleship**

**Week Four**

*The top two things Jesus taught me were…*

*I will follow, obey, and practice what He's taught me by…*

## The Top 2 Truths Jesus Has Taught Me About Discipleship

**Week Five**

*The top two things Jesus taught me were…*

*I will follow, obey, and practice what He's taught me by…*

**The Top 2 Truths Jesus Has Taught Me About Discipleship**

**Week Six**

*The top two things Jesus taught me were…*

*I will follow, obey, and practice what He's taught me by…*

**The Top 2 Truths Jesus Has Taught Me About Discipleship**

**Week Seven**

*The top two things Jesus taught me were…*

*I will follow, obey, and practice what He's taught me by…*

## ONE FINAL QUESTION

They were right in the big middle of their everyday routine. They were doing what they always did. Day in and day out, the rhythm of their lives revolved around fishing. But one day, Jesus interrupted their routine with an invitation. *Follow me.* From that moment on, they were changed. Their lives would never be the same again.

Seven weeks ago, you studied those same fishermen. Since that time, I wonder, has Jesus interrupted the everyday routine of your life with that same invitation? *Follow me.* As you have studied His Word over the past few weeks, I believe you have heard that invitation. My final question to you now as you conclude this study, precious sister, is this: **Are you a disciple?**

If your answer to that question is yes, I have one more thing for you to do before you close this workbook. Complete the sentence in the circle below by recording your name and today's date.

*are you a*
# DISCIPLE?

In response to Jesus' call to follow Him,

I ,_____ _____,

have accepted the invitation to become

His disciple on _____.

God bless you for studying God's Word with me. I love you, and this is my prayer for you:

*And now, just as you accepted Christ Jesus as your Lord, you must continue to follow him. Let your roots grow down into him, and let your lives be built on him. Then your faith will grow strong in the truth you were taught, and you will overflow with thankfulness.* — Colossians 2:6-7

Your sister in Christ,

*Laurie*

are you a DISCIPLE?

# At-a-glance Overview

### (FOR YOU & FOR THOSE YOU DISCIPLE)

**The Call of Christ:**

1) To Salvation: _____. *1 John 1:12, John 3:16*

2) To Discipleship: _____ _____. *Mark 1:16-17*

**The Cost of Discipleship:**

1) _____ _____. *Luke 9:23-24*

2) _____. *Luke 9:23*

3) _____ _____. *Luke 14:26*

4) _____. *Luke 14:33*

**The 7 Distinctives of Devoted Disciples:**

1) _____ and _____ God's Word. *John 8:31*

2) Free from their _____ _____. *John 8:32*

3) _____ and _____ by the Holy Spirit. *Acts 1:8*

4) _____ at all _____. *Luke 18:1*

5) _____ much _____. *John 15:8, Gal. 5:22-23*

6) _____ _____ for others. *John 13:34-35*

7) _____ character. *Luke 6:40*

**The Realities & Rewards of Discipleship:**

1) _____ and suffering. *John 15:20*

2) _____. *Luke 18:29-30*

**The Disciple's Mission:**

1) To _____ _____. *Matt. 28:19-20*

2) To be a _____. *Acts 18:1-6, 18-28, Rom. 16:3-5, 2 Tim. 4:19*

# Notes:

Week One

[1] Dietrich Bonhoeffer, *The Cost of Discipleship* (New York: Simon & Schuster 1995) 38.

[2] Louis A. Barbieri, *The Bible Knowledge Commentary: An Exposition of the Scriptures by Dallas Seminary Faculty*, ed. John Walvoord and Roy Zuck (Colorado Springs, CO: Cook Communications, 1985), WORDsearch CROSS e-book, 16.

[3] Ibid.

[4] Ibid.

[5] Oswald Chambers, *My Utmost for His Highest* (New York: Dodd, Mead & Company) 171.


Week Two

[1] J. Oswald Sanders, *Spiritual Discipleship: Principles of Following Christ for Every Believer* (Chicago, IL: Moody Press 1990, 1994) 8.

[2] Chad Brand, Charles Draper, Archie England, ed., *Holman Illustrated Bible Dictionary* (Nashville: Holman Bible Publishers, 2003), s.v. ",", WORDsearch CROSS e-book.

[3] Spiros Zodhiates, *The Complete Word Study Dictionary New Testament* (Chattanooga, TN: AMG Publishers, Revised edition 1993) 936.

[4] J. Oswald Sanders, *Spiritual Discipleship: Principles of Following Christ for Every Believer*, 8.

[5] Leadership Ministries Worldwide, *The Outline Bible Five Translation, Practical Word Studies in The New Testament* (Chattanooga: Leadership Ministries Worldwide, 1998), WORDsearch CROSS e-book, Under: "#1541: Follow".

[6] Spiros Zodhiates, *The Complete Word Study Dictionary New Testament*, 112.

[7] Adam Clarke, *A Commentary and Critical Notes* (New York: Abingdon-Cokesbury Press, 1826), WORDsearch CROSS e-book, Under: "1 Corinthians 3".

[8] Albert Barnes, *Notes on the New Testament Explanatory and Practical*, ed. Robert Frew WORDsearch CROSS e-book, Under: "1 Corinthians 3".

[9] Warren W. Wiersbe, *The Bible Exposition Commentary —New Testament, Volume 1* (Colorado Springs, CO: Victor, 2001), WORDsearch CROSS e-book, 577.

[10] J. Vernon McGee, *Thru the Bible with J. Vernon McGee* (Nashville, TN: Thomas Nelson, 1983), WORDsearch CROSS e-book, Under: "Chapter 4".

Week Three

[1] George Barna, *Growing True Disciples* (Colorado Springs, Colorado: WaterBrook Press, 2001) 114.

[2] Ibid., p. 169-170.

[3] Spiros Zodhiates, *The Complete Word Study Dictionary New Testament* (Chattanooga, TN: AMG Publishers, revised edition, 1993) 960.

[4] Barton B. Bruce et al., *Life Application New Testament Commentary* (Wheaton, IL: Tyndale Houseon, 2001), WORDsearch CROSS e-book, 411.

[5] Ibid.

[6] Zodhiates, *The Complete Word Study Dictionary New Testament*, 567.

[7] Warren W. Wiersbe, *The Bible Exposition Commentary – New Testament, Volume 1* (Colorado Springs, CO: Victor, 2001), WORDsearch CROSS e-book, 322.

[8] Lawrence O. Richards, *The Teacher's Commentary*, (Wheaton, IL: Victor Books, 1987), WORDsearch CROSS e-book, 729.

[9] R. C. Sproul, *The Heresy of Perfectionism*, Ligonier Ministries, http://www.ligonier.org/blog/heresy-perfectionism/.

Week Four

[1] Charles Stanley, *The Wonderful Spirit-Filled Life* (Nashville, TN: Thomas Nelson Publishers, 1992) 8.

[2] Ron Dunn, *Don't Just Stand There Pray Something* (San Bernadino, CA: Here's Life Publishers, Inc., 1991) 19-20.

Week Five

[1] Bruce Wilkinson, *Secrets of the Vine* (Sisters, Oregon: Multnomah Publishers, Inc., 2001) 105.

[2] Albert Barnes, *Notes on the New Testament Explanatory and Practical*, ed. Robert Frew WORD*search* CROSS e-book, Under: "John 15".

[3] Spiros Zodhiates, *The Complete Word Study Dictionary New Testament* (Chattanooga, TN: AMG Publishers, revised edition, 1993) 960.

[4] Ibid.

[5] Warren W. Wiersbe, *The Bible Exposition Commentary – New Testament, Volume 1* (Colorado Springs, CO: Victor, 2001), WORD*search* CROSS e-book, 355-356.

[6] Spiros Zodhiates, *The Complete Word Study New Testament* (Chattanooga, TN: AMG Publishers, 1992) 878.

[7] Ibid., 966.

[8] Ibid., 909.

[9] Ibid., 934.

[10] Ibid.

[11] Ibid., 967.

[12] Ibid., 878.

[13] Ibid., 947.

[14] Ibid.

[15] Spiros Zodhiates, *The Complete Word Study Dictionary New Testament*, 1208.

[16] Ibid., 499.

[17] Henrietta C Mears, *What the Bible is All About* (Ventura, CA: Regal Books, 1998), WORD*search* CROSS e-book, 432.

Week Six

[1] Lou [1]Spiros Zodhiates, The Complete Word Study Dictionary New Testament (Chattanooga, TN: AMG Publishers, Revised edition 1993) 1209.

[2] Ibid., 563.

[3] Ibid., 1468.

Week Seven

[1] Because discipleship is part of the process of sanctification, God is committed to discipling me (and you) until I draw my final breath and arrive on heaven's shores.

[2] Warren W. Wiersbe, *The Bible Exposition Commentary – New Testament, Volume 1* (Colorado Springs, CO: Victor, 2001), WORD*search* CROSS e-book, 107-108.

[3] Ibid.

# SHOP PRIORITY

Visit Priority's online store to find out more about Bible studies, DVDs, and CDs by Laurie Cole. Each product will encourage and equip you to give God priority.

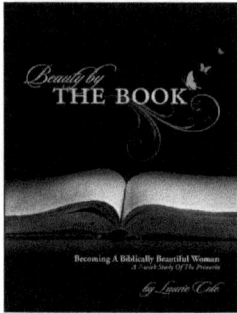

## Beauty by THE BOOK
**Bible Study**
Discover the do's and don'ts of Biblical beauty at any age in this practical 7-week study from Proverbs.

## Beauty by The Book *for Teens*
**Bible Study**
Learn what true beauty really looks like in this practical 7-week study from Proverbs.

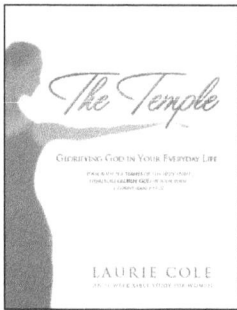

## The Temple
**Bible Study**
Priority's *"you glo, girl"* 11-week Bible study will help you discover how to *glo*–glorify God.

## There is a Season
**Bible Study**
An 11-week study for women, designed to help you experience contentment in every season of life.

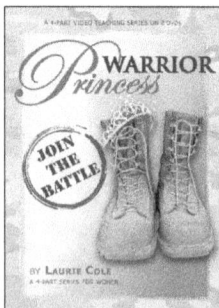

## WARRIOR Princess
**Video only, no homework Bible study.** Spiritual warfare is real, and you are on the front lines! Discover how to recognize and defeat your enemy.

## Audio CD sets and MP3 Downloadables

*Resources available for these studies:*
Workbooks, Small Group CD-ROM Leader Guides, Video Lectures, and Audio Lectures.

*Priority Ministries*
Encouraging Women to Give God Glory & Priority

# CONNECT WITH LAURIE AND PRIORITY

**Priority Ministries blog**

Encouraging Women to Give God Glory & Priority

The Priority blog is dedicated to busy women everywhere who may have a million things going on, but still want to make God the #1 thing. It can be done, and Laurie's guilt-free teaching and resources will help you do it. You really can give Him priority, even in your busy life!

**www.priorityministries.com/christian-womens-blog**

---

# SUPPORT PRIORITY

**Priority Partners**

Supporting Priority Ministries

*Priority Partners* believe in the mission of Priority Ministries and support it with their generous financial gifts. Would you prayerfully consider becoming a Partner and helping us reach and teach women to love God most and seek Him first?

Become a monthly or one-time donor. Either way, your financial gifts provide vital support for this ministry! For more information about becoming a Priority Partner, visit our website:

**www.priorityministries.com/donations**

*Priority Ministries is a non-profit 501(c)3 organization.*
*Your gift is tax deductible.*